all my love
Florence Vuk
Dec 2003

Prayers for Life

Contributing Writers:
Nancy Parker Brummett
June Eaton

pil

Publications International, Ltd.

Nancy Parker Brummett is an author and freelance writer living in Colorado Springs, Colorado. Her book credits include *Simply the Savior*, *The Journey of Elisa*, *It Takes a Home*, *Walk With Jesus*, and contributions to *Prayers for Good Times and Bad*.

June Eaton is a teacher and freelance writer who holds a master's degree from Northwestern University. Her previously published work includes Sunday school curriculum, stories, and articles in more than 50 Christian publications, plus contributions to nine books, including *A Mother's Daily Prayer Book*, *Prayers for Our Country*, and *This Too Shall Pass*.

Louis Weber, CEO
Publications International, Ltd.
7373 North Cicero Avenue
Lincolnwood, Illinois 60712

Manufactured in China.

8 7 6 5 4 3 2 1

ISBN: 0-7853-7507-4

Library of Congress Control Number: 2002107211

CONTENTS

❊   ❊   ❊

To Pray Is to Talk to God

❋   ❋   ❋

*F*OR MOST OF US, prayer arises out of the sincere longing of our soul to be in touch with our Creator. It can be a simple conversation with God, a deeply felt desire to immerse yourself in the presence of God, or perhaps a "telegram" sent to God in a sudden moment of need.

Prayer is time spent with God. There is no one right way or place to pray. You can pray sitting down, standing up, or lying in bed. You can pray before you eat or sleep, at the beginning of the day or at the end. You can pray moment by moment as you work or play, or as you stand in line at the supermarket.

You may shout your prayer, whisper it, or commune with God in absolute silence. You may put it to music and sing it, or write it in a private journal. Any time, anywhere, for any reason, it is appropriate to pray.

Prayers for Life is meant to bring you comfort, as well as to inspire and encourage you in your own prayer life. The book is composed of seven themes: celebration, encouragement, faith, comfort and healing, forgiveness, love, and peace. Each theme provides prayers, scripture verses, poetry, hymns, and quotes, all designed to help you draw closer to God.

These prayers and blessings come from the deepest places of the heart. They are written by people like you, offering thanks for the Lord's bountiful gifts and seeking his comfort. The words will help you connect with our awesome, approachable God.

To use *Prayers for Life,* find a place that is quiet and peaceful, where you can relax and be alone with God. Read the entries in order, or leaf through the book and find a chapter that meets a particular need.

After you have read and reflected upon the inspirational words offered in this book, take time to focus on your own situation. You may want to pour out your words to God in prayer, sharing your thoughts and feelings. Or, you may want to contemplate what you've read and wait quietly for his presence to fill you.

God hears you, and he answers you—through his Spirit, through his Word, or through the people in your life. Begin your journey now, and await your blessings!

CHAPTER 1

CELEBRATION

❋   ❋   ❋

For you shall go out in joy,
and be led back in peace;
the mountains and the hills
before you shall burst into song.

ISAIAH 55:12

. . . for in him all things in heaven
and on earth were created.

COLOSSIANS 1:16

❊   ❊   ❊

*L*ORD, TODAY *I celebrate your glorious creation. You have formed
the day and the night, the sun and the moon, the earth and the
seas. You have brought into being plants and animals of every
kind—and you have made me. You have formed me from the dust
of the earth, and you have breathed into me the breath of life.*

*In infinite detail you have created your world, and you have
pronounced it "good." Your beauty and handiwork surrounds
me daily. I thank you for each star, each leaf, each gleaming
drop of life-giving water—each point of wonder in your world.
Creator God, make me worthy of these gifts.*

❊   ❊   ❊

At the dawn of creation, God laid
out his plans for the universe, and
the plan is still working.

Let the heavens be glad, and let the earth rejoice; let the sea roar, and all that fills it.

PSALM 96:11

❊　　❊　　❊

FATHER IN HEAVEN, I praise you for the splendor of spring. The heaven and earth have a new song to sing as they rejoice in the awakening of nature. Your people, too, awake to the glories of living in your world as the new season beckons. I thank you, Lord, for the beauty of the earth, for your love and care, and for new life.

❊　　❊　　❊

What love fills our hearts when spring kisses us on the cheek!

This is the day that the Lord has made;
let us rejoice and be glad in it.

PSALM 118:24

❊ ❊ ❊

*H*EAVENLY FATHER, *as I face a new day with you at my side, I remember that this is a day you have given me, free and clear. It is a clean slate upon which I can write my life's song. I give you thanks for this day: for your continued presence, for your goodness, and for your enduring love.*

Even though things may not go perfectly today, I know you are with me. You are my strength and my refuge, my help in time of trouble. Wrap your arms around me, Lord, so I can meet this day in perfect confidence and joy.

❊ ❊ ❊

The dawn of a new day brings new
possibilities and challenges. We hope
they'll all be good ones, but we know they
won't, and that's where God comes in.

THE SLATE IS clean, Lord, the calendar as bare as the Christmas tree. Bless the New Year that beckons. We sing of you as help in ages past, but we need to know you as hope for years to come. Help us face what we must, celebrate every triumph we can, and make the changes we need. We're celebrating to the fullest this whistle-blowing, toast-raising moment, for it is the threshold between the old and the new us.

It is God's gift that all should eat and
drink and take pleasure in their toil.

ECCLESIASTES 3:13

❄   ❄   ❄

*F*ATHER, IN THESE *days of uncertainty and joblessness, I thank you
for the meaningful work you have given me. In your wisdom, you
have furnished me with tasks that help me use my skills and satisfied
my longing to serve you. Through the years, you have made each of
my jobs suitable in its time. I know the pleasures I enjoy are gifts
from a loving God to his loving child, and I accept them with
gratitude. Keep me close to you, Lord, so I may continue to celebrate
and take pleasure in the ordinary daily activities of my life.*

But we had to celebrate and rejoice,
because this brother of yours was
dead and has come to life; he was
lost and has been found.

Luke 15:32

❋   ❋   ❋

*L*ORD, ONE OF *the saddest times for parents comes when a young son or daughter becomes alienated from the family. Anger and resentment flare up and compound the anguish. It is a situation that happens all too often.*

I ask you to comfort the parents, Father, and fill the void in their hearts with thoughts of your love and goodness. Help them to be patient and open to opportunities for reconciliation. Reach down to comfort and protect their beloved child as well, and soften the hearts of all involved, until the joyful day when the lost is found and the celebration begins.

Gray hair is a crown of glory;
it is gained in a righteous life.

PROVERBS 31:28

✳ ✳ ✳

*I THANK YOU for my mother's life, Father.
I thank you for her steady influence, for
her even temperament, and for her
unfailing love. She has taught me by
example how to live a life anchored in
you, and she has shown me what it
means to give one's self in the service of
others. Though she is old, your light has
not gone out of her eyes. Continue to
bless her all of her days, until the time
she celebrates with you in heaven.*

I will sing to the Lord as long as
I live; I will sing praise to my
God while I have my being.

Psalm 104:33

❁   ❁   ❁

Dear God, I praise you for your gift of music. Music is not only a gift and a source of joy but also a means of worship. How can I thank you enough for giving me such delight? Grant me, I pray, the pleasure of celebrating you in song as long as I have breath.

❁   ❁   ❁

Music is the soul's celebration of life.

I will bless those who bless you, and the one
who curses you I will curse; and in you all
the families of the earth shall be blessed.

GENESIS 12:3

❋   ❋   ❋

FATHER OF ALL, you have favored me with the greatest
blessing in my life—my family. Long ago you promised
this blessing to us through your servant Abraham. I
did not know when I read your promise how much
the blessing would mean.

Thank you for the trust you have placed in me and
for the deep love both given and received. My family
has brought my life meaning and fulfillment beyond
all I would have imagined. As my children build their
own families, be with them, Lord, and pass on the
blessing to them.

Thanks be to God, who gives us the
victory through our Lord Jesus Christ.

1 Corinthians 15:57

❋　　　❋　　　❋

*L*ORD, ARE VICTORIES *to be won only in sports or in battle, or can*
we experience them daily, in small ways, throughout our lives?

For a tiny child, victory may be that first word spoken or the first
step taken. For an elderly arthritic, victory may be tasted just in
getting out of bed in the morning or putting one foot in front of
the other to walk.

For me, victory has meant learning to make a fresh loaf of bread
and filling my hours with meaningful activity. Each day you give
victory over the darker sides of our nature as you fill us with your
love. I celebrate the power of that love, to change us and to
conquer all adversity.

❋　　　❋　　　❋

Victory is to conquer that which
we once thought impossible.

BLESS THE COUPLE *before you, Lord, with the best marriage has to share: peace, not of a stagnant pond, but of deep rivers flowing; strength, not of sheltered dogwood, but of oak, sycamore, and beech, storm-tossed and rooted; power, not of fists and temper, but of seedlings stretching toward the sun.*

I am bringing you good news of
great joy for all the people. . . .

LUKE 2:10

❊   ❊   ❊

*F*ATHER, WHO WOULD *not rejoice over the good news of a long-awaited new life in the family? The birth of a child is a cause for celebration—one of the greatest joys you give us. Thank you for blessing us all in this way.*

My heart soars as I anticipate welcoming this child into our family. Please watch over the mother-to-be, Lord. Keep her healthy and safe, just as you protected your servant, Mary.

Thank you for giving this young woman the opportunity and the privilege to become a part of your creation. Make her worthy of your trust in her and help her to be the kind of parent you want her to be. Above all, let her know that you are always at her side.

❊   ❊   ❊

To become a mother is to
learn the language of love.

*B*LESS THIS LITTLE *one of so few days.*

May the child be prosperous in every way.

Healthy in body and mind,

Growing strong and kind.

Bless this little one through all the days.

There is no greater mystery than love, Lord of covenants and promises. We are in its presence on this anniversary day. Bless those who live, day after ordinary day, within the fullness of married love, surely one of the greatest mysteries. Bless them as they honor their past, even while they create a future. Let them bask in the pleasures and applause of today, when we bow before their accomplishments, which are an inspiration and blessing to us all.

See! The winter is past;
the rains are over and gone.
Flowers appear on the earth;
the season of singing has come,
the cooing of doves
is heard in our land.
The fig tree forms its early fruit;
the blossoming vines spread their
   fragrance.
Arise, come, my darling,
my beautiful one, come with me.

       Song of Solomon 2:11–13 NIV

❋   ❋   ❋

Thank you, Lord, for our marriage. Like a wedding band, our love encircles but doesn't bind. Like a vow, our love is words but sustains because of what they mean. In your grace, our love has the permanence of rock, not of walls, but of a bridge to moments ahead as special and bright as when we first met.

Let marriage be held in honor by all.

HEBREWS 13:4

❋   ❋   ❋

*CREATOR OF US ALL, since Eden you have put
your stamp of approval on the sacred state of
marriage, and shown us how two can become
one. We continue to celebrate the rite of marriage
in our families and among friends, just as your Son
celebrated the wedding at Cana.*

*Even more do we celebrate the longevity of the
partnerships blessed by you, Lord, and marked
with fidelity, love, and support for one another. We
love only because you have given us the capacity to
love. We love, because you first loved us.*

❋   ❋   ❋

Love is freely giving the self in
service of another.

WE GATHER THIS day around a table of celebration,
shouting welcome and "Hosanna!" Yet, as children do in
play when given palm fronds as tokens of remembrance,
we so quickly turn them into swords. Take away our love
of violence, our way of creating weapons from peaceable
moments. And for us at this table, God of lions and
lambs, heal any hurt feelings, saddened hearts, and
lonely days so that we can truly celebrate being together
this day in a crowd of friends and family. We have a long
week ahead before we celebrate again.

WE ARE CELEBRATING Easter today,
O God. Join us as we gather to share
a meal, giving thanks for the angel
rolling away the stone. Bless those at
this table savoring the food and the
message of this day. Remind us, too,
Lord of unexpected appearances, that
this also is the season of spring, a time
when rebirth is not so surprising after
all. After lunch send us outside into the
yard where, hiding colored Easter eggs for
the children, we may understand anew
what this day really means.

Two are better than one.... For if they
fall, one will lift up the other.

ECCLESIASTES 4:9–10

❊   ❊   ❊

*BLESS MY FRIENDS, O Lord! What joy they bring
to me. Bless the ones I see every day and those I
can easily connect with after a long separation.
Bless the ones I laugh with and the ones who cry
with me. Bless the friends of my youth and of my
middle age, Lord, and please send me more
friends to accompany me in old age. It was so
gracious of you to give me friends, Lord. Touch
each one in a special way today. Amen.*

❊   ❊   ❊

. . . to get full value of a joy you must
have somebody to divide it with.

MARK TWAIN

Every generous act of giving, with every perfect gift, is from above, coming down from the Father of lights.

JAMES 1:17

*A*LMIGHTY FATHER, *you've placed so many things in our world purely to bring us joy: ice cream cones and popcorn; juicy oranges, icy lemonade, and warm cocoa; kitten tricks and puppy licks; watermelon and fireworks! For all those wondrous things, we celebrate you!*

God keeps them occupied with the joy
of their hearts.

ECCLESIASTES 5:20

❊ ❊ ❊

*L*ORD, *HOW DELIGHTED* *we are by an unexpected visit from a*
butterfly. We were in awe when we learned the process that trans-
forms the lowly caterpillar into the exquisite winged creature. But
in studying the life expectancy of the butterfly, we are reminded
how fleeting and fragile life can be. Let every butterfly I see remind
me that our time on this earth is limited, too. Help me remember
that the person I have an opportunity to be kind to today, the one
I allow an extra measure of grace, might not be in my life at all
when tomorrow comes. May I see every life as a fragile and
precious gift to be appreciated and cherished today.

❊ ❊ ❊

We find in the flight of butterfly wings
A message about more glorious things:
Take time to care, take time to smile,
For you, too, may linger for just awhile.

Lead me in the path of your commandments, for I delight in it.

PSALM 119:35

❊ ❊ ❊

DEAR GOD, *I don't take the joy of walking
for granted. I know there are those without
the physical strength, the desire, or the
energy to exercise. So I begin my walk by
thanking you that on this day you have
granted all three to me. Walking in the
direction you would have me go is how I
want to walk, Lord. Show me the paths
and turns you would have me take in this
lifelong walk with you. Amen.*

O sing to the Lord a new song,
for he has done marvelous things.

PSALM 98:1

❄   ❄   ❄

*F*ATHER GOD, IT'S *so easy for us to become distracted from the real purpose of life, which is to glorify you and enjoy you forever! You have created us in your magnificent image, a reflection of all that is good and holy. Fill us with the spirit of worship, Lord, that we may sing and shout for joy from this day forth. Amen.*

In his hand is the life of every living thing
and the breath of every human being.

JOB 12:10

❊   ❊   ❊

*GOD OF ALL creation, I never cease to
be amazed by the work of your hands.
Today, when I look outside and see the
glories of the day beginning to emerge,
I am reminded of all the ways you are
working to restore me and to bring me
into the light, too. Thank you, Lord, for
caring enough about me to consistently
renew me and to give me hope that each
day I live is a day worth celebrating.
I'm glad my life is in your hands.*

Light is sweet, and it is pleasant
for the eyes to see the sun.

ECCLESIASTES 11:7

❀   ❀   ❀

WHAT A BLESSING it is to walk in the warmth
of the sunshine! Help me to be aware of your
many gifts to us. Because, whether it is a gray
cloud or a rainbow, it is from you.

*L*ORD, *WHAT JOY you* send into the world when you grace us by sending a new baby! These little ones seem to have the light of heaven in their eyes from the moment we gaze upon them. As small as they are, they can make grown men cry and women weep with joy, and they make everyone feel that life is worth living all over again. Babies are such completely innocent, joyful blessings. No wonder you chose to send your own son to earth in the form of a newborn baby. We praise you for him and for all the babies born to us before and since.

✤   ✤   ✤

To hold a new baby is to believe in miracles.

ALMIGHTY GOD, WHEN *we see you in creation, we worship you as Creator. When we see you in forgiveness, we worship you as Forgiver. When we see you in our provision, we worship you as Provider. When we see you in our lives, we worship you as Lord. In all ways, for all our days, we worship you! Amen.*

❀   ❀   ❀

O worship the King, all glorious above,
O gratefully sing His power and His love.

ROBERT GRANT

SKIPPING UP THE *sidewalk . . . first day of school.*
Reading, writing, 'rithmetic.

First steps, first dates, first jobs. Hurrying down the
sidewalk, diploma in hand . . . last day of school.

What more can I say, dear God, than I've said since
before my beloved graduate was born? Watch over
and visit this young person with your presence.
We've done a pretty good job so far, you and I—and
now it's time to let go.

Be with me. I'm better at roots than wings. Remind
me that nothing can separate us from one another
or your love. Help me be there for my children as
you are for me, companion God. Go with this child
today. I mustn't follow too closely, and I can't yet
judge my distance.

In him we live and move and have our being.

ACTS 17:28

❊　　❊　　❊

*L*ORD, THANK YOU *for this extended family you've placed me in. I know that none of us are here by accident, even though it may seem as if we're a strange collection of personalities at times! Still, we are all here by your choice and for your reasons. Help us appreciate one another for our uniqueness, Lord, but let us also find strength in holding hands in a circle of faith. For it is you who created us and put us together. We thank you for bringing us together as family—and we praise you for welcoming us into your family.*

❊　　❊　　❊

Families are circles of love in which no one wants to be the first to let go of someone else's hand.

I thank my God every time I remember you, constantly praying with joy in every one of my prayers for all of you.

PHILIPPIANS 1:3–4

❊ ❊ ❊

*T*ODAY, LORD, *we honor the grandparents who tended us so well. Pause with us as we play again in the dusty lanes of childhood at Grandma and Grandpa's house. Bless these bigger-than-life companions who helped us bridge home and away, childhood and maturity. In their footsteps, we made the journey. Thank you for such heritage and a day on which to express our gratitude.*

WITH BOLDNESS and wonder and expectation, I greet you this morning, God of sunrise and gleaming dew. Gratefully, I look back to all that was good yesterday and, in hope, I face forward, ready for today.

The sun does not shine for a few trees and flowers, but for the wide world's joy.

HENRY WARD BEECHER

Happy birthday to you!
That was a good day, and you were there.
Everyone who saw you thought:
"How beautiful!"
So take a moment in front of the mirror:
"Still beautiful!"
For God sees only your loveliness,
From day one.

❋　　❋　　❋

Thanksgiving is nothing if not a
glad and reverent lifting of the
heart to God in honour and praise
for His goodness.

James R. Miller

*B*LESS THIS CANDLELIT *festival of birthday celebration, Lord, for our special loved one. Join us as we blow out candles and joke about setting the cake ablaze, about golden ages and silver hairs. Our laughter is bubbling up from gratitude that the years are only enriching this special celebrant. We are grateful that the years are enriching our lives as friends and family as well.*

THIS BIRTHDAY, Lord, I can see that my child is becoming a grown-up. Surely it's just the smoke from all those candles making me cry. But, Lord, wasn't it just yesterday that there was only one candle? From before that day to this, I've trusted you. I ask you now to bless the youthful drive to risk making choices; the struggle to be heard; the changing body, moods, and mind. Bless—and this is hardest for me to say—the urge for independence. Bless me with ears to listen, a shoulder to lean on, and the good sense to build bridges, not walls.

The joy of Jerusalem was heard far away.

NEHEMIAH 12:43

❊   ❊   ❊

Your word, Lord, tells us of the many celebrations that were held when Israel returned from exile. From the restoration of the temple, to the rebuilding of the wall around Jerusalem, we learn that each was a cause for celebration.

My cause for celebration is my church. In love and gratitude, I thank you, Father, for this house of worship. The church is more than just a building. The church is a body of people with diverse gifts, each member contributing to the whole. This body offers me support, sharing, and caring. None of us is perfect, because perfection dwells only in you, O Lord. But with your help, we give each other the best we have to offer.

In love, I pledge myself in service to you, Holy Father, and to my fellow members.

So much to celebrate, Lord: *waking to dawn gilding trees; squeezing fresh orange juice, its zest clinging to my hands all day; making a new friend, talking to an old one; watching the first leaf bud, raking the last. Each day's turning brings gifts from you to celebrate.*

❊   ❊   ❊

Lord, may I be wakeful at sunrise to begin
    a new day for you,
cheerful at sunset for having done my work
    for you;
thankful at moonrise and under starshine
    for the beauty of the universe.
And may I add what little may be in me to
    your great world.

THE ABBOT OF GREVE

WE GATHER AROUND this feasting table, humbled by our bounty, Lord of abundant life; we have so much more than we need. We confess that we are poised, fork in hand, ready to overdo. Help us learn better how to live as grateful, if overstuffed, children— delighted, surprised, and generous with the sharing of our good fortune. Bless us now as we enjoy it amidst food, friends, and family. We give the heartiest thanks for your diligent, steadfast care.

You crown the year with your bounty; . . .
The pastures of the wilderness overflow, . . .
the meadows clothe themselves with flocks,
the valleys deck themselves with grain, they
shout and sing together for joy.

PSALM 65:11–13

❅   ❅   ❅

*BLESS US IN this time of good fortune.
Give us the grace to be grateful for new-
found comforts, magnanimous among
those who have less, and thoroughly
giving with all we've been given. Amen.*

O Lord, you are my God; I will exalt
you, I will praise your name; for you
have done wonderful things.

ISAIAH 25:1

❊　　❊　　❊

*I PRAISE YOU, Almighty God, for your
wisdom, and for your promise to bury
your laws in our hearts and minds that
we might be wise, too! Thank you for
your Holy Word, Lord, for in it we can
find the truth. Give us your discernment,
O God, that we might always walk as
wise followers of the only all-wise God.
Amen.*

❊　　❊　　❊

The greatest good is wisdom.

ST. AUGUSTINE

I will call to mind the deeds of the
Lord; I will remember your wonders
of old. I will meditate on all your
work, and muse on your mighty deeds.

PSALM 77:11–12

❊   ❊   ❊

*CONNECTED IN MEMORY to holidays past,
like links in a colorful paper chain decorating
the tree, we begin another advent. Some
recollections are happy and pleasant, others
sad and empty, yet each brings us to this new
starting point, as fresh and full of promise as
an egg about to hatch at Easter. Make all
things new this holiday, even old memories,
for this is the season of second chances.*

*You ARE A WELCOME guest at this table,
God, as we pause in the midst of this
bell-ringing, carol-making season of too
much to do. Send us your gift of silent
nights so that we can hear and know
what you will be bringing us this year: yet
another gift of hope. Bless our gathering
around this table; we will set a place
each day for you. Join us in our daily
feast, for which we now give thanks.*

❄   ❄   ❄

[Tim] told me, coming home, that he
hoped the people saw him in the church,
because he was a cripple, and it might be
pleasant for them to remember upon
Christmas Day who made lame beggars
walk, and blind men see.

CHARLES DICKENS

In the beginning was the Word, and the
Word was with God, and the Word was God.

JOHN 1:1

✳   ✳   ✳

*MAY WE REJOICE in the written Word.
The Scriptures can come alive for us;
only take, and read. Discover the acts of
God in history. Travel with his disciples
along the pathway of service. See how
his church began, how it grew through
the centuries. Yes, celebrate the written
Word, for it is a mirror of, and a witness
to, the Living Word of the heavens.*

To us a child is born, to us a
son is given. . . . And he will be
called Prince of Peace.

ISAIAH 9:6

❄   ❄   ❄

*W*E ARE SUCH *stubborn folk, God, only moving toward you*
when it's time for a baby's birthday! What an illogical story,
yet you knew it would take something unexpected to get our
attention. Be with us as we edge toward the manger again
this year, both from curiosity and habit, pausing to kneel
there because we are finally getting the message.

As servants of God, we have commended ourselves in every way: . . . by purity, knowledge, patience, kindness, holiness of spirit, genuine love.

2 CORINTHIANS 6:4,6

❋　　❋　　❋

*L*ORD, HELP US *be ready to offer your gentle touch today—and celebrate the gift of kindness. We can reach out to the elderly and infirm. Stretch out our hands to the children and infants. Remind us not to hold back. Help us celebrate by letting your warmth flow through. We will rejoice in our ability to do your will, God, in this way.*

❋　　❋　　❋

God puts something good and loveable in every [person] His hands create.

MARK TWAIN

You have turned my mourning into dancing; . . . and clothed me with joy.

PSALM 30:11

❊ ❊ ❊

LORD, I HAVE cried out to you for help, and in your mercy, you have heard me. Throughout the long night of my loved one's illness, I prayed and you answered my prayers. You gave me strength, you restored my soul, you brought healing. In the light of morning, my heart danced for joy. Heavenly Father, my Lord and my helper, I give thanks and praise to you forever.

Thou, my all! My theme!
My inspiration! and my crown!
My strength in age—my rise in low estate!
My soul's ambition, pleasure,
wealth!—my world! My light in darkness!
and my life in death!
My boast through time! bliss through
    eternity! Eternity, too short to speak thy praise!
Or fathom thy profound love to man!

        Edward Young, *Night Thoughts,* "Night IV"

I will proclaim your name to my
brothers and sisters, in the midst of the
congregation I will praise you.

HEBREWS 2:12

❈　　❈　　❈

MAY THE BLESSING of God fill our days.
Especially, may we develop the perfect
balance of duties to family and respon-
sibilities at work and worship. As we seek
serenity in these things, may we find
great cause for celebration, knowing
that the one who loves us unconditionally
remains at the center of all our activity.

Joyful, joyful, we adore thee, God of glory,
　　Lord of love;
hearts unfold like flow'rs before thee,
op'ning to the sun above.
Melt the clouds of sin and sadness,
drive the dark of doubt away;
giver of immortal gladness, fill us with the light
　　of day.

All thy works with joy surround thee,
earth and heav'n reflect thy rays,
stars and angels sing around thee,
center of unbroken praise.
Field and forest, vale and mountain,
flowery meadow, flashing sea,
chanting bird and flowing fountain,
call us to rejoice in thee.

HENRY VAN DYKE

*L*ORD, *I* THANK *you for the joy you bring me
each day
for the trials that test my joy,
for the comfort you give me when I'm tested,
for the love you show when you comfort me,
for the joy I feel, knowing I'm loved by you.
Lord, I thank you.
Amen.*

❈   ❈   ❈

When I think of God, my heart
is so full of joy that the notes leap
and dance as they leave my pen:
and since God has given me a
cheerful heart, I serve him with a
cheerful spirit.

FRANZ JOSEPH HAYDN

For now we see in a mirror, dimly, but
then we will see face to face. Now I know
only in part; then I will know fully.

1 CORINTHIANS 13:12

❁   ❁   ❁

*S*OMETIMES UNDERSTANDING *eludes me, Father, when I pray for*
help and you seem far away or seem not to care. But in your own
good time, and in your own way—not mine—your answer comes.
Often it is far from what I had expected. Most of the time it is far
better than the solution my feeble brain had envisioned. So now I
am patient and trust you to care for my tiny world, and when
understanding comes, I rejoice!

Let us rejoice and exult
and give him the glory.
REVELATION 19:7

❄ ❄ ❄

O LORD, *I savor this triumph: I met my goal!*
Day by day, I reached into my heart and found
   energy to keep on.
Day by day, I reached out and found your hand
   leading, your inspiration guiding. Stand with
   me to accept applause for our joint success.

❄ ❄ ❄

The Way of Heaven does not compete,
and yet it skillfully achieves victory. It
does not speak, and yet it skillfully
responds to things.

LAO-TZU

The Lord has established his throne in the heavens, and his kingdom rules over all.

PSALM 103:19

✸   ✸   ✸

It is one thing for us to realize, God, that you made everything we see in our world, but how awesome it is to stop and consider that what we can see is just one small part of your whole creation. You are the God of heaven and earth and of all things beyond our galaxy. You rule all the kingdoms of this universe with your wisdom, power, and authority. I bow before your greatness, O God.

CHAPTER 2

ENCOURAGEMENT

✳   ✳   ✳

Do not be frightened or dismayed,
for the Lord your God is with you
wherever you go.

JOSHUA 1:9

And we urge you, beloved, . . . encourage the faint hearted, help the weak, be patient with all of them.

1 Thessalonians 5:14

❊   ❊   ❊

Lord, help me to be an encourager. Help me to sense when others are hesitant and fearful, so I can give them the support they need.

I, too, need encouragement when I am afraid or my confidence flags, or when I am uncertain whether my decisions are correct. Then I long to hear your voice whispering: "Don't be afraid—I am with you."

I will turn the darkness before them into
light, the rough places into level ground.

ISAIAH 42:16

❄   ❄   ❄

*L*ORD, WHEN WE *have nothing left to hold on to,*
you provide us with hope as an anchor for our
souls. We need that hope now, and we pray that you
will fill every broken place in our hearts with its
reassuring light. Thank you, Lord, for in you we
have an unending supply of hope in the midst of
uncertainty and failure. We know that if we could
see this situation through your eyes, we would see
how you will bring us through it.

We place our hope in you and you only. Amen.

❄   ❄   ❄

I would rather walk with God in
the dark than go alone in the light.
MARY GARDINER BRAINARD, *Not Knowing*

*L*ORD, *I* WANT *the encouragement I get from you to go through me to others I love. Show me how to pray for them, Lord, that they might receive so much of your heavenly encouragement that their cups are overflowing! Teach me to respect each person I love for who they are in your eyes, Lord. And may all my prayers for them be a great encouragement to them. Amen.*

One song can spark a moment,
One flower can wake the dream.
One tree can start a forest,
One bird can herald spring.

One smile begins a friendship,
One hand clasp lifts a soul.
One star can guide a ship at sea,
One word can frame the goal.

One vote can change a nation,
One sunbeam lights a room.
One candle wipes out darkness,
One laugh will conquer gloom.

AUTHOR UNKNOWN, "ONE"

IT SEEMS UNCANNY, God, how many times people have been in just the right place, at just the right time, with just the right word or touch as I've struggled through experiences. I can't help but believe that somehow you've had a hand in all those chance encounters. It makes me feel special that you would bother to arrange such specific and meaningful moments of care for me, and I just want to let you know that I'm grateful.

❅　　　❅　　　❅

When you have no helpers, see all your helpers in God. When you have many helpers, see God in all your helpers. When you have nothing but God, see all in God; when you have everything, see God in everything. Under all conditions, stay thy heart only on the Lord.

CHARLES HADDON SPURGEON

And when you turn to the right or when you turn
to the left, your ears shall hear a word behind
you, saying, "This is the way; walk in it."

ISAIAH 30:21

❋   ❋   ❋

*IN THE EARLY light of morning, I bid you come, Lord, and we meet
the day together. You show me the way I should go, and I follow.*

*You walk before me, making my way smooth, steering my course,
inspiring courage.*

*You quiet the voices of self-doubt and bring comfort and healing.
You give me strength to face the tasks at hand. You provide food
for my body, nourishment for my mind.*

*Your help is endless, Heavenly Father. You never abandon me. And
when daylight fades, you give me rest. How great you are, O God.*

❋   ❋   ❋

We make our own plans, but it is God who leads
the way and clears the obstacles from our path.

The Lord will keep you from all evil; he will keep your life. The Lord will keep your going out and your coming in from this time on and forevermore.

Psalm 121:7–8

❄   ❄   ❄

Lord, I'm feeling discouraged today. I know you will see me through this time, but I ask that you also give me your clarity of thought, your wisdom, and your peace. Then I will be able to keep everything that is concerning me in your perspective. Thank you so much for caring for me so deeply that you never leave me alone. In your name I pray. Amen.

He replied, "Truly I tell you, today
you will be with me in Paradise."

Luke 23:43

❋　　❋　　❋

*HEAVENLY FATHER, of all your promises, the
promise of paradise and the return to the splendor
of Eden is the most spectacular.*

*The thought of spending eternity in nothingness is
bleak at best. But in your compassion, you have
given us the hope that those who are your faithful
children will one day join you in heaven.*

*Death will lose its hold on us. Illness and sorrow
will be banished. Time will have no meaning.
Only peace and harmony will reign. Thank you,
precious God, for this comforting message.*

Look at the birds of the air; they neither sow nor reap nor gather into barns, and yet your heavenly Father feeds them. Are you not of more value than they?

MATTHEW 6:26

❋   ❋   ❋

LORD, I CONFESS *that I am a worrier. I look at a situation and see everything that is wrong with me instead of the many things that are right.*

You discourage me from such negative thinking and remind me that I am valuable in your eyes and that you will take care of me.

Free me from this lack of trust in my own value, Father, and in your willingness to provide for me. Help me to see myself as I really am: a child in need, with a loving father.

I want their hearts to be encouraged and united in love.

Colossians 2:2

❋   ❋   ❋

Almighty God, what an encouragement it is to us that you placed us all in families. Having a family means there's always somebody to turn to in good times and bad. Having a family means we know we will be loved even when we make a mess of our lives. I ask you to make me more grateful for the family I have been given, Lord. Please remind me not to take those in my family for granted but to always see them as the unique individuals you created them to be. Help me see that each person in my family, no matter how old or young, has a special contribution to make to the rest of us, and that being together makes us all stronger than we would be alone. Thank you, Lord, for families. Amen.

❋   ❋   ❋

Bless this family, Lord.
This is my fervent prayer.
Hold us safely in your arms
And sustain us by your care.

BLESS ALL THE MOTHERS *and fathers today, Lord. Grant them those little moments of pure surprise and joy that encourage them, and remind them there is no greater job, no nobler love, than being a parent. Please place in their hearts the knowledge that each second is fleeting. Help them to realize the now. I ask all this in your precious name. Amen.*

❊ ❊ ❊

Nothing can compare in beauty and wonder and admirableness, and divinity itself, to the silent work in obscure dwellings of faithful women bringing their children to honor, virtue, and holiness.

HENRY WARD BEECHER

My Lord and my God, I thank you for sending your loving people to me with words of praise and encouragement when I most need them. Sometimes it is difficult to continue without some clue, some kind of reassurance that I am succeeding in what I am trying to accomplish.

Everyone needs to be appreciated, and I need to do my part. Please help me to build up my family and friends in the same way, so they, too, can be encouraged.

❊ ❊ ❊

Without praise, the soul withers.

Therefore encourage one another and build
up each other, as indeed you are doing.

1 Thessalonians 5:11

❋   ❋   ❋

*L*ORD, HELP ME *know when I need to encourage a friend. So
often I'm so focused on the ups and downs of my own life that I
fail to notice when someone looks more tired than usual or has a
worried look in her eyes. It takes so little to encourage someone,
Lord. I know that, but sometimes I forget.*

*Help me to see the need to encourage, Lord, in times of great
need and on a daily basis. Amen.*

With us is the Lord our God, to
help us and to fight our battles.

2 Chronicles 32:8

❄   ❄   ❄

We know there is no greater burden than
to think no one cares or understands. That
is why the promise of your presence is so
precious to us, you who said: "Remember, I
am with you always, to the end of the age."

❄   ❄   ❄

Lighten our darkness, Lord, we pray; and in
your mercy defend us from all perils and dangers of this night; for the love of your only
Son, our Saviour Jesus Christ. Amen.

Gelasian Sacramentary, "An Evening Prayer"

But you shall worship the Lord
your God; he will deliver you out
of the hand of all your enemies.

2 Kings 17:39

❈　　❈　　❈

Heavenly Father, humans have harmed other humans since the beginning of time. I have often been naive and felt untouchable. But now I know that human enemies are ever-present, fueled by hate, envy, and greed. They are real, and they are unpredictable. To them, personal innocence is irrelevant.

Lord, take away my sense of panic and feeling of powerlessness in the face of such an enemy. Help me to remember that you are an all-powerful God and you are still in charge.

Put on the whole armor of God, so
that you may be able to stand
against the wiles of the devil.

EPHESIANS 6:11

✼　　✼　　✼

*WE'RE TOLD THAT just as sure as sparks fly
upward, humans are born to trouble (Job 5:7).
Instead of being naturally good, as you intended,
Lord, your people are born into sin. When we see
unprovoked meanness and ugliness in the world,
we can well believe it.*

*But we are not without protection, for you have
told us we can put on your armor. You have given
us the armor of truthfulness, right living, faith,
and peace. With your help, O Lord, we can
conquer our sinful natures.*

We are afflicted in every way, but not crushed; perplexed, but not driven to despair; persecuted, but not forsaken; struck down, but not destroyed.

2 Corinthians 4:8–9

❋   ❋   ❋

How difficult it must have been, Father, to maintain hope in the face of persecution and frustration as the early Christians did. What fortitude they displayed.

Sometimes when I feel beaten down, I think of those people, battling against the odds from every direction. It was their faith in you that made the difference.

Strengthen my faith like that, Lord, so I will not be crushed nor driven to despair. Help me to find hope.

Those who go out weeping, bearing the seed for sowing, shall come home with shouts of joy, carrying their sheaves.

PSALM 126:6

❅   ❅   ❅

*Y*OUR WORD, LORD, *tells us that those who sow in sorrow will reap in joy. For the Israelites this meant that no matter how much trouble occurred during planting, the harvest would bring happiness. I thank you, Father, for this message of hope. I look forward to my harvest of joy that will follow sorrow.*

The Lord has anointed me; he has sent
me to bring good news to the oppressed,
to bind up the brokenhearted...

ISAIAH 61:1

Amazing grace!
How sweet the sound
That saved a wretch like me;
I once was lost, but now I'm found;
Was blind, but now I see.

'Twas grace that taught my heart to fear,
And grace my fears relieved;
How precious did that grace appear
The hour I first believed.

Through many dangers, toils and snares
I have already come,
"'Tis grace that brought me safe thus far,
And grace will lead me home.

JOHN NEWTON, "AMAZING GRACE"

I FEEL ALONE and forlorn, Lord. I see the sunshine outside but I don't feel its warmth. I see birds in the trees but I don't hear them sing. I turn to you. Please hear me and help me to break out of this despair. Give me strength to become aware of the blessings I have in my life. Help me to shift my attention from my present circumstances and focus on your eternal love for me.

❋   ❋   ❋

There are joys which long to be ours. God sends ten thousand truths, which come about us like birds seeking inlet; but we are shut up to them, and so they bring us nothing, but sit and sing a while upon the roof and then fly away.

HENRY WARD BEECHER, *Life Thoughts*

*L*ORD, GIVE ME *the faith to take the next step, even when I don't know what lies ahead. Give me the assurance that even if I stumble and fall, you'll pick me up and put me back on the path. And give me the confidence that, even if I lose faith, you will never lose me. Amen.*

FATHER, WHEN I AM feeling weak and vulnerable, I like to read the psalms that depict you as a shepherd and me as the sheep. Thank you for the soothing image of rest in cool, green fields and beside life-giving waters.

It is a reassuring thought that a shepherd, no matter how large his flock, will relentlessly search for a lost sheep until it is found.

As my shepherd, you consider me just as important as every other sheep in your fold. I find comfort in knowing that you will watch over all my needs and come looking for me when I am lost.

WHEN FACING a difficult job, I often panic, Father.
My heart pounds, my throat constricts, and anxiety
takes over, rendering me nearly useless. Then I turn
to thoughts of you, Lord, as the source of my help.

At first I think, "Is this a task too small for you?
Should I even bother you with such minor problems?"
But my answer comes, born of past experience: There
is no concern too small or too large for the Lord.

My breathing slows and my body relaxes as I put
myself in your hands. Bit by bit, the work gets done,
and I offer you my profound gratitude. How blessed
I am to have a God like you!

❉   ❉   ❉

Taking a deep breath is good medicine,
providing you breathe in the breath of God.

So teach us to count our days
that we may gain a wise heart.

PSALM 90:12

❄ ❄ ❄

*L*ORD, *IT'S HARD growing older sometimes. We may falsely begin
to think it's too late to make a difference. Whenever I begin to
feel like I'm too old to change the world for you, I remember
what you did in just three years, Lord Jesus. With your strength in
me I can do all things! Please use my time for your glory. Amen.*

LORD, I WISH TO *live a long life,*

but I fear growing old.

I want to accomplish great things,

but I fear risking what I already have.

I desire to love with all my heart,

but the prospect of self-revelation makes me shrink back.

Perhaps for just this day,

you would help me reach out?

Let me bypass these dreads and see instead

your hand reaching back to mine—

right now—just as it always has.

❄   ❄   ❄

I would not give one moment of
heaven for all the joys and riches of
the world, even if it lasted for thousands and thousands of years.

MARTIN LUTHER

There's hope for your future, says the Lord.

JEREMIAH 31:17

❊　　　❊　　　❊

WHAT A BLESSING to have a second chance! Grant me the wisdom to use this opportunity wisely. And save me from the fear that I'll fall into the same old traps as last time. This is a brand-new day, a whole new beginning. Thank you, Lord, for not losing hope for me.

❊　　　❊　　　❊

Father, I abandon myself into your hands;
　　do with me what you will.
Whatever you may do, I thank you:
I am ready for all, I accept all.
Let only your will be done in me, and in
　　all your creatures—
I wish no more than this, O Lord.

CHARLES DE FOUCAULD, "PRAYER OF ABANDONMENT"

I AM GRATEFUL, *God of Hope, for the gift of each new day, each new season, like the one unfolding around me now in flower and birdsong, in seedling and bud. When they arrive as surely as dawn follows night and bloom follows bulb, I am uplifted by the fulfillment of your promise.*

In the shadow of your wings I will take refuge ...

PSALM 57:1

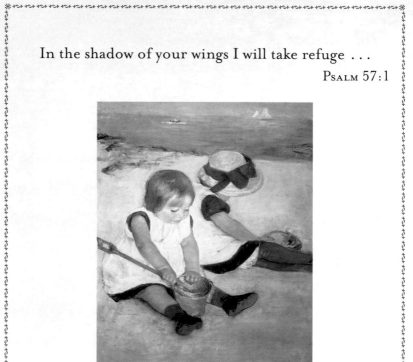

Like a little child in trouble,
I searched for a place to hide,
Until the storms of life would pass me by.
But no place was deep enough, strong enough,
    safe enough, to shield me from danger.
Only the shadow of your wings, dear Lord,
Could provide the shelter I require.

God is our refuge and strength,
a very present help in trouble.
Therefore we will not fear.

Psalm 46:1-2

❁   ❁   ❁

HOW I LOVE the sound of those words, Heavenly Father: "God is our refuge and strength." Just reading them makes me feel stronger.

Troubles bombard me from every direction in this stressful world, Lord, but your word reassures me that you are always ready and willing to provide me with a place of refuge, a haven from the storms of life. To all who love you, you promise your strength to help face demons and subdue them. With that kind of support, how can I be afraid?

❁   ❁   ❁

The only place of true safety is in God's arms.

*L*ORD, *I* AM *facing a difficult situation today.*
Please be present with me and help me
to hear your voice above all the rest.
Give me strength and wisdom and a
double dose of your wondrous love.
Thank you, and amen.

Those who wait for the Lord shall renew their strength, they shall mount up with wings like eagles, they shall run and not be weary, they shall walk and not faint.

Isaiah 40:31

❊   ❊   ❊

THE LAYOFF IS ice in my mind. Who am I now? What can I do? This is all I've done. The questions range the pay scale, for being laid off, Lord, is an equal opportunity ambush. As I wait to be called back, inspire me to make my job that of hunting another job. Somewhere I'll be needed again. Please stand with me while I wait.

Bless our attempts at success,
Lord, though we know some of them
will end in failure. We pray that you
will even bless our failures, for we
also know that never risking is a sign
of apathy and a questioning of
your constant goodwill toward us.

❋   ❋   ❋

I believe sympathy is one of the
most helpful helps one can bestow
upon one's fellow creatures; and it
seems a great pity that so many
people feel it is their duty to criti-
cize rather than sympathize.

HANNAH WHITEHALL SMITH

O LORD, HEAR MY prayer for all who are in trouble
this day.

Encourage those who are finding it difficult to believe in
the future and doubting the truth of your existence
or the validity of your promises.

Let your hope fill their hearts as they recall all your past
faithfulness.

Bring wise friends into their lives who have long known
the reality of your love.

Let them be assured that you can take care of every need,
no matter how large or small. Amen.

Return to the Lord, your God, for he is
gracious and merciful, slow to anger,
and abounding in steadfast love.

JOEL 2:13

❊   ❊   ❊

*SOMETIMES I DO hurtful things, Father. Then, all
around me, people become angry with me, and I
wonder if you are angry, too.*

*But when I go to you, confessing my faults and
weaknesses, you do not chide me. Instead, you are
full of grace and mercy, offering your love.*

*Help me to be more like you, Lord, treating others
as you treat me: forgiving when they err against me,
becoming gracious in my attitude toward them, and
offering love instead of anger.*

❊   ❊   ❊

When it seems like God is treating
you like a favorite child, that's grace.

For in Christ Jesus you are all children of God through faith. . . . There is no longer Jew or Greek, there is no longer slave or free, there is no longer male and female; for all of you are one in Christ Jesus.

GALATIANS 3:26,28

❄ ❄ ❄

OPPOSITES DON'T attract nearly as often as they repel, if we are to believe the headlines. Pick a race, color, creed, or lifestyle, Lord of all, and we'll find something to fight about. Deliver us from stereotypes. Inspire us to notice value in everyone we meet. As we dodge the curses and hatred, we are relieved there is room for all beneath your wings. Bless our diversity; may it flourish.

And the peace of God, which surpasses all understanding, will guard your hearts and your minds.

Philippians 4:7

❊   ❊   ❊

These are mean-spirited times, and we quake and shudder. Tend us, loving Creator, and shelter us in the palm of your hand against all that would uproot and destroy us. We are the flowers of your field.

❊   ❊   ❊

In His will is our peace.

Dante Alighieri
The Divine Comedy

I am longing to see you so that . . . we may be mutually encouraged by each other's faith.

ROMANS 1:11–12

❊ ❊ ❊

*B*LESS OUR DIFFERENCES, *O Lord. And let us love across all barriers: the walls we build of color, and culture, and language.*

Let us turn our eyes upward and remember that you, the God who made us all, live and breathe and move within us, untouched by our petty distinctions. Let us love you as you are for you love us just as we are.

God, give me joy in the common things;
In the dawn that lures, the eve that sings.

In the new grass sparkling after rain,
In the late wind's wild and weird refrain;
In the springtime's spacious field of gold,
In the precious light by winter doled.

God, give me joy in the love of friends,
In their dear home talk as summer ends;
In the songs of children, unrestrained;
In the sober wisdom age has gained.

God, give me joy in the tasks that press,
In the memories that burn and bless;
In the thought that life has love to spend,
In the faith that God's at journey's end.

God, give me hope for each day that springs,
God, give me joy in the common things!

Thomas Curtis Clark

Humble yourselves before the
Lord, and he will exalt you.

JAMES 4:10

❊   ❊   ❊

LORD, GIVE ME courage to admit my mistakes,
apologize, and go on. Keep me from getting
stuck in denial, despair, and, worst of all, fear
of trying again. In your remolding hands, God
of grace, failures can become feedback and
mistakes can simply be lessons in what doesn't
work. Remind me that perfection means
"suited to the task," not "without mistakes."
There's a world of difference.

❊   ❊   ❊

Man errs so long as he strives.
JOHANN WOLFGANG VON GOETHE, *Faust*

Yet, O Lord, you are our Father; we
are the clay, and you are our potter;
we are all the work of your hand.

Isaiah 64:8

❊   ❊   ❊

*GOD OF MERCY, this week seems to be pulling me in
so many different directions I don't know what mat-
ters anymore. Please shape me, mold me, and smooth
out all my jagged edges that I might once again be of
some use to myself, to others, and to you. Amen.*

*L*ORD, COULD YOU *please send one of your cleansing rains and your sweeping winds through my house today? You see, it needs a good cleaning and I haven't the time or the energy to do it. Give me a heart of gratitude for the home I have, Lord, and show me how to keep my thoughts focused on you as I work. Let me know that when I please my family by providing a clean home for them to enjoy, I'm also pleasing you.*

❄   ❄   ❄

May He support us all the day long, till the shades lengthen, and the evening comes, and the busy world is hushed, and the fever of life is over, and our work is done! Then in His mercy may He give us a safe lodging, and a holy rest, and peace at the last.

JOHN HENRY NEWMAN
Sermons Bearing on Subjects of the Day

*I WANT TO help and encourage my
family, God, but sometimes my ideas
of how to help are misunderstood.*

*Please grant me wisdom and discernment
to know what will work best for each
person in each unique situation.*

*Help me remember that listening
is the first step toward having an
understanding heart.*

*And remind me to use humor when I
need to keep things in perspective.*

❋   ❋   ❋

You are one among many. Hear others'
words so that they may hear your own.

Therefore a man leaves his father
and his mother and clings to his
wife, and they become one flesh.

GENESIS 2:24

*L*ORD, *IN EVERY MARRIAGE there are gaps and spaces that
occur due to differences in personalities or experiences. Try
as we might, we can't truly be united as one unless you
surround us with your Holy Spirit and fill every empty space.
We pray for you to bless our marriage. Fill it with your
presence that we might be fully and wholly united. Amen.*

BLESS US IN this time of transition.

May we use the time wisely

to consider our shortcomings,

to seek ways to amend our faults,

and to reconnect with a deeper love.

❊ ❊ ❊

Winds of change blow fierce when we
forget to anchor our hearts in God.

MAN OF SORROWS, *see my grieving heart this day. Keep me from feelings of shame, though, as I let the loss wash over me. For this is a part of my life, too, the life only you could give me: to learn what it means to let go.*

❈　　❈　　❈

Seeking courage, Lord,
　　I bundle my fears
　　and place them in your hands.
Too heavy for me,
　　too weighty even to ponder
　　in this moment.
Such shadowy terrors shrink
　　to size in my mind
　　and—how wonderful!—
wither to nothing in your grasp.

Do not be afraid of sudden panic, or of the storm that strikes the wicked; for the Lord will be your confidence.

PROVERBS 3:25–26

❃   ❃   ❃

IT ISN'T EASY to make a life transition, but, God, this one seems especially difficult. I'm trying to be brave, but there is so much uncertainty, and I lack confidence in my ability to successfully adjust to my new situation. Please walk me through this change, step by step. Help me to not cling stubbornly to the past nor to try looking too far into the future. Where my self-confidence ends, let my confidence in you begin.

The wind blows where it chooses, and you
hear the sound of it, but you do not know
where it comes from or where it is going.
So it is with everyone born of the Spirit.

JOHN 3:8

❄   ❄   ❄

*If I LAUNCH myself in a new direction
or into uncharted waters, God, will
you guide me? Please surround me
with your powerful spirit, for without
it I could never get under way. I'm
not afraid to climb in the boat, Lord,
but my courage comes always, and
only, from you. Please be the wind
in my sails. Amen.*

MAY I BE ASSURED *of your presence, God, as I weather this storm. As the waves toss me about and the ship of life threatens to crash into rough rocks: You are there. I won't despair. For no wind or water, rock or sand has the power to defeat your plans for me. After all, you created these things, and in you alone they have their existence.*

God moves in a mysterious way,
His wonders to perform;
He plants his footsteps in the sea,
And rides upon the storm.

WILLIAM COWPER, *Olney Hymns*

O GOD, HOW GRACIOUS it is of you to create heaven to encourage us. Because we know we have an eternal home with you, we don't have to worry about our earthly homes falling down around us. Because we know we will have new bodies, free of disease and suffering, we can rejoice in our afflictions. And because we know we will be reunited with loved ones who go before us, we have a heavenly hope. Sometimes we feel like strangers on this earth, Lord, for we know that heaven is our real home. Thank you for encouraging us by showing us glimpses of heaven here on earth—in a sunset or a child's smile—so we can fully anticipate the glory to come. Amen.

❋ ❋ ❋

God's in his heaven—all's right with the world!

ROBERT BROWNING

Jesus answered her, "If you knew the gift of God, and who it is that is saying to you, 'Give me a drink,' you would have asked him, and he would have given you living water."

JOHN 4:10

LORD, *YOUR LIVING WATER* *blesses and sustains us. Let it flow over all whose hearts are breaking and soothe their troubled souls. Let it spring up around those who are discouraged and lift them closer to you. Send your living water rolling into our lives wave after powerful wave, filling us with the sweet satisfaction of your spirit. Amen.*

Because the Lord God helps me, I
will not be dismayed; therefore, I
have set my face like flint to do his
will, and I know that I will triumph.

Isaiah 50:7 TLB

❅   ❅   ❅

A problem and a promise—
God does not leave us unarmed.
He has made a way of escape;
he will not have us harmed.
Persevere in obedience—
he may be testing our faith.
But he will lead us victoriously
to arrive at our promised place.

CHAPTER 3

FAITH

❈ ❈ ❈

*If I take the wings of the morning
and settle at the farthest limits of
the sea, even there your hand
shall lead me, and your right
hand shall hold me fast.*

PSALM 139:10

Now faith is the assurance of things hoped for, the conviction of things not seen.

HEBREWS 11:1

❄   ❄   ❄

THANK YOU, FATHER, for the faith of those in my family who went before me and who first put my feet on the path to knowing you. I confess that I cannot see you or touch you or hear you (maybe sometimes I hear you in the form of my conscience), but I know you are there. The evidence of your love and care for me is just too strong to be discounted.

Thank you for the blessings of faith in my life. Continue to strengthen my knowledge of you and help me pass on my faith to my children.

❄   ❄   ❄

Action, not words, is the best witness that faith can have.

Faith is knowing without seeing,
believing without fully understanding,
trusting without touching
the One who is ever faithful.

Why are you afraid?
Have you still no faith?

MARK 4:40

❊   ❊   ❊

THE DISCIPLES lost their nerve on a storm–tossed boat, Peter had doubts in his quest to walk on water, and I worry a lot, Lord. We each have our weak moments and our regrets afterward. I need help with my weakness, Father. Worry destroys my sleep, my peace of mind, my health, and it solves no problems.

Reach out your hand to me, Lord, as you did to Peter. Calm the wind and waves of doubt in my heart as you did for the disciples. Strengthen my assurance of your love and care so I may find your peace.

❊   ❊   ❊

Worry and fear are robbers, taking from us those things that are not yet missing.

By faith Noah, warned by God about
events as yet unseen, respected the warning
and built an ark to save his household.

HEBREWS 11:7

❋   ❋   ❋

*N*OAH OPENED *himself up to ridicule by building a huge,
clumsy boat in the middle of the dry season. But he did it,
Lord, following your instructions down to the last detail.*

*I want to be like Noah: strong and wise and full of faith.
Unfortunately, I'm just me: weak and foolish and full of
fear. But with just a glimmer of faith, I know that you have
the power to make the weak strong and give courage to those
who are afraid. I know it because I have seen it happen.
Lord, give me that kind of strength and courage and wisdom
for the task I have ahead. In your name, I can succeed.*

❋   ❋   ❋

God can help you do the thing you fear to do.

I can do all things through
him who strengthens me.

PHILIPPIANS 4:13

❊   ❊   ❊

My grandmother has a "can-do" spirit.
She has your strength, Father, and she continues
to accomplish what younger people have ceased
to try. Thank you for her example, Lord. When
I am her age, I hope that my faith will beat as
strongly in my breast—that I will still reach
for you and lean on you for my support.

❊   ❊   ❊

A strong spirit can overcome
even the weakest flesh.

Show yourself in all respects
a model of good works.

TITUS 2:7

✾   ✾   ✾

*M*Y DAD WAS *someone I could count on, Lord, to*
support our family, to love us, and to take care of
us. He is the reason I can believe in you, Father
God. You provided him as a model of your love and
care, and through him I can know you.

Thank you for my dad. He helped build up my faith
and made it possible for me to believe in you, and to
know you love me and will take care of me forever.

✾   ✾   ✾

When a parent leads the way
to God, children follow.

If you do not stand firm in faith,
you shall not stand at all.

ISAIAH 7:9

❋   ❋   ❋

*L*ORD, *I* HOPE *if I'm asked about my faith in you that I can state it with quiet confidence or shout it from the rooftops: My God has created the world! He has created me. He loves me and watches over me and forgives my sins. He is almighty. He can do anything!*

I know your rising up and your sitting down, your going out and coming in.

Isaiah 37:28

❄   ❄   ❄

A FELLOW AIRLINE passenger arrogantly declared to me that you don't exist, Father. This person believed only in money, power, and modern technology. But when the money and power are gone, and technology breaks down, will this person cry out to you? I can have faith in modern technology only because I have faith in you, Lord. To you I am not a nameless, faceless creature. I am your child and you watch over me. You are the source of my confidence. Amen.

Stand firm and hold fast to the
traditions that you were taught.

2 Thessalonians 2:15

❄   ❄   ❄

THE CHILD I'VE LOVED and nurtured has suddenly lost his faith. He grew up in the church. Our lives revolved around you and your church, Father. The Lord's Prayer and the creeds came easily to his lips. All the familiar words and hymns have been imprinted on his soul, but now the core of his faith is gone. He seems lost and aimless without the rudder you provided him.

Reach down, O God, and reclaim this child you made your own. Touch his heart. Help him feel the fullness of your grace. Pull him back to you and to our family, and make him whole again.

Look you scoffers! Be amazed and perish, for in
your days I am doing a work, a work that you
will never believe, even if someone tells you.

ACTS 13:41

I PLACE MY CONFIDENCE *in you, almighty God. You have brought
beauty and order to the world by your plan. You have created life
that develops in a precise pattern, not out of chaos, but out of
love. Love created the world. Love's name is God!*

But blessed are your eyes, for they
see, and your ears, for they hear.

MATTHEW 13:16

✳   ✳   ✳

OPEN MY HEART'S *eyes, Lord,*
  so I can see you.
Open my heart's ears, Lord,
  so I can hear you.
Open my mind, Lord, so I can understand
  the glory and wonder of your love.
You touch me in my sorrow. You heal
  my pain. You give me courage.
Mold me in your image, Lord,
  so I can serve you in love. Amen.

My grace is sufficient for you.
2 CORINTHIANS 12:9

❊   ❊   ❊

GRACE, AMAZING grace, is your gift to me, Heavenly Father. Though I am a sinner, you have saved me from eternal death. You have shown me your mercy and forgiven me. Because you have pardoned my sins, I am a new person in your eyes, Lord. You shower me with your favor and bless me daily. Though I am still weak, your grace lives in me and strengthens me. How did I ever merit such love?

So faith comes from what is heard.

ROMANS 10:17

❋   ❋   ❋

My GRANDMA often read her leather Bible, with pages as thin as tissue. She nourished herself with your Word, Lord, often reading aloud to me. Some things I didn't understand then, and some I still don't comprehend. But her faith rubbed off on me, Father, and I nourish it just as she did, using that same Bible, as well as my own. Guide me through your Word, Lord, so I can grow a faith as strong as hers.

❋   ❋   ❋

The more I read my Bible, the
more I see myself within its pages.

We will not all die, but we will all be changed, in a moment, in the twinkling of an eye, at the last trumpet.

1 Corinthians 15:51

❊   ❊   ❊

Lord, you have left us with a mystery. It is the mystery of the ages: What will happen on the last day? What is heaven like?

These questions are followed by so many others as we ponder the "how" and the "what" of that final trumpet call.

My feeble imagination cannot envision that change—in the twinkling of an eye—into a spiritual body instead of a physical one. But it doesn't matter. I will bear your image and bask in your light, and the "how" and "what" will have to be a surprise.

Declare his glory among the nations,
his marvelous works among all the
peoples. For great is the Lord and
greatly to be praised.

Psalm 96:3–4

❋   ❋   ❋

*God of Heaven and Earth, the longer I
live and the more I learn, the more I am awed
by the complexity of your creation. With
revelation of each new scientific discovery,
my wonder grows. Scientists may think they
are inventing, but they are merely reporting
and revealing the depth of your intricate
works. I sing praises to you, Lord. You are
the King of the universe; all praise and
glory to your name. Amen.*

Wisdom makes one's face shine.
ECCLESIASTES 8:1

❊ ❊ ❊

IT'S BECOME too easy, Lord, to ask you for your blessing on our meal, or your grace to get us from home to work, or for an opportunity to say hello to a neighbor. Your hand is in all these things, and we ask for your intervention because we need it. Help me to recognize that I am asking the Lord of all things to participate in my life. I want to know it in my head as well as my heart.

❊ ❊ ❊

Faith thrives when we stay focused
on God rather than on ourselves.

CREATOR OF ALL THINGS, I'm so thankful for angels. You have dispatched those majestic beings that flock around you in holy worship to earth; it is almost too marvelous for me to imagine. Surround those I love with angels, Lord. Please send one to stand at the foot of the bed of each precious child in our family. Assign one to each car on the road and each plane in the sky. Bless us with your angels, Lord. They are welcome among us.

❋　　　❋　　　❋

I face each day with certainty
And sleep without a fear,
For I know the Lord of Heaven
Has an angel standing near.

*L*ORD, *SO OFTEN we find it easier to give to others than to receive from them. Yet Jesus allowed others to provide for his needs often, including accepting a cool drink of water from the Samaritan woman at the well. Don't let me be too proud to receive help, time, or gifts from others, Lord. Help me to be a gracious receiver as well as a generous giver so others may be blessed by giving to me. Amen.*

※　　　※　　　※

To receive a gift graciously is to bring joy to the giver.

I believe; help my unbelief!

MARK 9:24

❊　　❊　　❊

*G*OD, FAITH CAN SEEM *so illusive at times. We want to believe and yet the cares of the world are distracting. I thank you that with one simple prayer, I came to believe, and I ask that others would, too. Prepare the hearts and minds of those who will hear your word in the days to come. Temper their intellect and pride so they will not be prevented from taking that simple step of faith. Thank you, Lord, for putting faith in my heart to stay—sealed by the Holy Spirit. I ask you to do the same for those who are struggling without you. Help their unbelief, Lord, and give them the unwavering faith they so desire.*

May the words of my mouth and
the meditation of my heart be
pleasing in your sight, O Lord,
my Rock and my Redeemer.

PSALM 19:14

✢   ✢   ✢

*L*ORD, *LIKE THE* A*POSTLE* Paul, I so often
do those things I would rather not do and
fail to do what I should. Any action, any
word I speak that is not edifying to others is
outside your will. Any task I leave undone
might be a missed opportunity for me to do
your work on earth. But you know me as no
one else can. Thank you for loving me in
spite of myself—for seeing not who I am,
but who you will bring me to be. Amen.

Draw near to God, and he will draw near to you.

JAMES 4:8

❊   ❊   ❊

HOW ENCOURAGING IT IS, O God, to know there are no obstacles at all keeping us out of your presence. All we need is faith—and all we have to do is enter in.

Faith—is the Pierless Bridge
Supporting what We see
Unto the Scene that We do not.

EMILY DICKINSON

O Lord, in the morning you hear
my voice; in the morning I plead my
case to you, and watch.

PSALM 5:3

❊   ❊   ❊

*THERE IS A QUIETNESS, a holiness about
the early morning hours that I want to
share with you. Before my household is
stirring, as I listen to the first birds
twittering outside my kitchen window
and the sound of coffee percolating, my
heart desires more than anything else to
enter into your presence. Come, dear
Lord. Meet me in the morning and let
us plan our day together. In your
precious name, I pray. Amen.*

*L*ORD, *I FEEL so close to you when I'm gardening. When I turn over a spade of dirt and see a big fat worm tilling up the soil, or when a ladybug on the back of a leaf catches my eye, I reflect once again on all the miracles of creation you have placed in our world. I'm reminded that I have to keep the weeds out of my life as well as out of my petunias, and that I am as dependent on your living water as my peas are on the water from my watering can.*

Thank you for this earth, Lord, and for the way you provide beauty through flowers and nourishment through vegetables. I see you at work in my garden, and I feel blessed. Amen.

❊   ❊   ❊

The kiss of the sun for pardon,
The song of the birds for mirth,
One is nearer God's heart in a garden
Than anywhere else on earth.

AUTHOR UNKNOWN

I DON'T THINK I've always lived my life focusing on the right things. Too often I'm going my own way without turning to you. So, with your help, Lord, for the rest of my life I'm going to pray before I lose precious time worrying. I'm going to find time to visit with babies and butterflies, or to sit on the steps sipping tea watching your world go by. For the rest of my life, Lord, I'm going to trust that you are always at work in all things, and I'll give you thanks long before my prayers are answered. I'm going to let go of living the hours of each day my way, and simply follow your lead. By your grace, this is how I will live—for the rest of my life.

❊   ❊   ❊

Our days are only worth living when
the Lord is the director of them.

Let us hold fast to the confession of
our hope without wavering, for he
who has promised is faithful.

HEBREWS 10:23

❊   ❊   ❊

*LORD, I WANT to change the world for
you! I want to create mountains of faith
for all to see! But I don't do that, Lord.
Instead, I seem to be content to con-
tribute just one small pebble at a time.
Please keep me faithful in piling up my
pebbles, so that someday they will
become a monument to you. Amen.*

❊   ❊   ❊

By faithfully living our small lives,
we can make a great difference.

WHAT SHALL WE DO today, Lord? Your agenda is the one I want to follow. Please look at my "to do" list and mark out those things that don't really need to be done today. And then, Lord, write in those things you would like for me to do instead. I believe that if I could see my day through your eyes, my plans would be entirely different. Guide me today, Lord. I give this day wholly to you.

I don't want to do it all today, Lord. I want to leave undone that which fails to serve you, and leave unsaid that which fails to glorify you.

I'VE TRIED TO plant seeds of faith in the lives of others, Lord, I really have. But so often I get discouraged because I don't see those seeds taking root and growing.

In fact, if I come back to check how they are doing, I may see only weeds. Help me remember that it may not be your will for these seeds to grow in my garden where I can see them. Help me realize that even when the seeds I've planted are growing somewhere else, I must still keep praying for sunshine and rain. And someday, by your grace, I may see your beautiful harvest in the lives of those in whom I planted seeds. Amen.

❋ ❋ ❋

But with every deed you are sowing a seed,
though the harvest you may not see.

ELLA WHEELER WILCOX

LORD, IT'S HARD to keep from projecting too far into the future. I begin to worry about things that I can neither determine nor change. But you have promised to be a light unto my feet, Lord. That light lets me see where to take my next step but doesn't let me see the whole path stretching in front of me. I know I can trust you to take me into the future one step at a time. Please give me strength and direction enough for today, Lord, and I'll leave the future up to you.

❊   ❊   ❊

I don't know what the future holds,
but I know who holds the future.

*M*Y MAIN GOAL IN *life is to follow you, Lord. If I lag too far behind or get distracted, please wait for me. For I know that if I lose sight of you, I am lost, and nothing about my life will have any significance. Thank you for asking me to follow you. I come. Amen.*

Just as I am, without one plea
but that Thy blood was shed for me,
And that Thou bidd'st me come to Thee,
O Lamb of God, I come! I come!

CHARLOTTE ELLIOTT

We know that all things work together
for good for those who love God, who
are called according to his purpose.

ROMANS 8:28

❈   ❈   ❈

*LORD, IT'S EASY for me to believe that all things
work together for good when things are going well.
Other times, I find it harder to hold on to the faith
that even those things will be used for good in your
hands. Yet it's precisely because I can't understand
that I believe. Thank you for your incredible
promise that you will take everything that happens
in my life, stitch it together like so many pieces of a
quilt, and create something beautiful of it. All
things work together for good in your hands
because you are good. May your goodness be
evident in the world as it is in my heart.*

I can do all things through him
who strengthens me.

PHILIPPIANS 4:13

❋   ❋   ❋

*L*ORD, YOU MUST GET *very discouraged by my lack
of faith sometimes. When will I ever learn that
whenever a task seems too big for me to do well and
on time, it seems that way because I fail to take into
consideration your participation? What I can't
possibly do on my own I can easily do when I ask
you to partner with me. Then it's almost as if all I
have to do is get out of the way so you, with your
awesome power and endless creativity, can make
your way known. Thank you, Lord, for reminding
me that there is no such thing as an impossible task
when you are by my side. Amen.*

Without faith, we are as stained
glass windows in the dark.

Author Unknown

These trials are only to test your
faith, to see whether or not it is
strong and pure. It is being
tested as fire tests gold and puri-
fies it—and your faith is far more
precious to God than mere gold;
so if your faith remains strong
after being tried in the test tube
of fiery trials, it will bring you
much praise and glory and
honor on the day of his return.

1 PETER 1:7 TLB

Do not believe them, though
they speak friendly words to you.

JEREMIAH 12:6

❋   ❋   ❋

Somebody said that it couldn't be done,
But he with a chuckle replied
That "maybe it couldn't" but he would be one
Who wouldn't say so till he'd tried.
So he buckled right in with the trace of a grin
On his face. If he worried he hid it.
He started to sing as he tackled the thing
That couldn't be done, and he did it.

There are thousands to tell you it cannot be done,
There are thousands who prophesy failure;
There are thousands to point out to you one by one,
The dangers that wait to assail you.
But just buckle in with a bit of a grin,
Just take off your coat and go to it;
Just start in to sing as you tackle the thing
That "cannot be done," and you'll do it.

EDGAR GUEST, *The Path to Home*

Sometimes I'm like Peter, and I walk on water.
I stand above my circumstances, which are like
    the swirling tempests of the sea.
But then, like Peter, I take my eyes off Jesus
    and concentrate on things below.
Soon I start to sink.
How I long to have a consistent, water-walking,
    eyes-on-Jesus faith.

I've been driven many times to my knees by the over-
whelming conviction that I had nowhere else to go.

ABRAHAM LINCOLN

Those of us who are strong and able in the faith need to step in and lend a hand to those who falter, and not just do what is most convenient for us.

ROMANS 15:1 *The Message*

❊   ❊   ❊

No matter what my ears may hear
Or what my eyes may see,
There's nothing for me to fear, Lord;
You're always here with me.

Lord, I am here.
> But child, I look for you
> Elsewhere and nearer me.
Lord, that way moans a wide insatiate sea:
How can I come to You?
> Set foot on the water, test and see
> If you can come to me.
Could you not send a boat to carry me,
Or dolphin swimming free?

> Nay, boat nor fish if your will fails you:
> For My Will too is free.
O Lord, I am afraid.
> Take hold on me:
> I am stronger than the sea.
Save, Lord, I perish.
> I have hold of you.
> I made and rule the sea.
> I bring you to the haven where you
> want to be.

CHRISTINA ROSSETTI, "CHRIST OUR ALL IN ALL"

I KNOW GROWING OLDER doesn't necessitate letting go of faith, Lord. Even though our bodies are getting more frail and our thinking may not be as sharp as it once was, dear God, you are still the same. We can always depend on you.

❄   ❄   ❄

Faith is believing what you do not see; the reward of faith is to see what you believe.

ST. AUGUSTINE

The root of faith produces the flower of heart-joy. We may not at the first rejoice, but it comes in due time. We trust the Lord when we are sad, and in due season He so answers our confidence that our faith turns to fruition and we rejoice in the Lord. Doubt breeds distress, but trust means joy in the long run. . . .

Let us meditate upon the Lord's holy name, that we may trust Him the better and rejoice the more readily. He is in character holy, just, true, gracious, faithful and unchanging. Is not such a God to be trusted? He is all-wise, almighty, and everywhere present; can we not cheerfully rely on Him? . . . They that know thy name will trust thee; and they that trust thee will rejoice in thee, O Lord.

CHARLES SPURGEON, *Faith's Checkbook*

*L*ORD, THE MORE *I learn about you, the more I
love you. And the more I love you, the more I want
to change the world for you. I want to create
mountains of faith for all to see, but I hear you
telling me that I need to be content to build those
mountains one small pebble at a time. Please keep
me faithful in the little things, Lord, that you might
be greatly praised. In Jesus' name, amen.*

❊   ❊   ❊

My faith looks up to thee
Thou Lamb of Calvary,
Savior Divine
Now hear me while I pray;
Take all my guilt away
O let me from this day
be wholly Thine.

RAY PALMER

I ACCEPT YOUR invitation to pray without ceasing. Hear me as I pray boldly, with expectation, believing your assurance that we deserve to be in your presence and to talk all we want. I am grateful that you welcome me at all times and in all places and moods. God, you are faithful; you will not let me be tempted beyond what I can bear.

Faith is the highest passion in a human being. Many in every generation may not come that far, but none comes further.

SØREN KIERKEGAARD

Be kind to your little children, Lord.

Be a gentle teacher, patient with our weakness and stupidity.

And give us the strength and discernment to do what you tell us, and so grow in your likeness. May we all live in the peace that comes from you.

May we journey towards your city, sailing through the waters of sin untouched by the waves, borne serenely along by the Holy Spirit.

Night and day may we give you praise and thanks, because you have shown us that all things belong to you, and all blessings are gifts from you.

To you, the essence of wisdom, the foundation of truth, be glory for evermore.

Clement of Alexandria, *To the Divine Tutor*

Examine yourselves to see whether
you are living in the faith.

2 Corinthians 13:5

❊　　　❊　　　❊

God grant me the joy of learning as I seek spiritual direction.

Help me to listen to those who are wise in the ways of the spirit,

as well as to hear the inner workings of my own heart.

And help me to grow closer to you, Lord. Amen.

THE DAY HAS BEEN LONG, LORD, but that's water under the bridge. Bless me now with stillness and sleep. I sigh and turn over, knowing that night will usher in the day with new joys and possibilities, gifts from your ever-wakeful spirit.

❊　　　❊　　　❊

Yet, in the maddening maze of things,
And tossed by storm and flood,
To one fixed trust my spirit clings;
I know that God is good! . . .
I know not where His islands lift
Their fronded palms in air;
I only know I cannot drift
Beyond His love and care.

JOHN GREENLEAF WHITTIER
"THE ETERNAL GOODNESS"

We are always confident . . . for
we walk by faith, not by sight.

2 Corinthians 5:6–7

*M*AY I COME TO *know that you are my friend, God. When I feel a frowning face is looking down upon me from heaven, I should recall that nothing I could do could ever make you love me more or love me less. You simply love—completely, perfectly. I will feel the blessedness of that!*

❋   ❋   ❋

Lord, dismiss us with thy blessing,
Hope, and comfort from above;
Let us each, thy peace possessing,
Triumph in redeeming love.

ROBERT HAWKER, "BENEDICTION"

LORD, MAY I KNOW that a wisdom and a love transcend the things I will see and touch today; that I walk in this light each step of the way. May I never forget that there is more to this existence than the material side of things—and be blessed when I suddenly become aware of it: in the smile of a child, in the recognition of my own soul's existence, and in the longing for immortality.

❀   ❀   ❀

Love of self for self's sake
Love of God for self's sake
Love of God for God's sake
Love of self for God's sake.

ST. BERNARD OF CLAIRVAUX,
FOUR STAGES OF GROWTH IN
CHRISTIAN MATURITY

For by grace you have been saved through faith, and this is not your own doing; it is the gift of God.

EPHESIANS 2:8

I COME TO CHURCH TODAY, *not because of duty or because a preacher calls, but because you, O God, invite me, your child, for whom you've been searching. In the words and songs, the lights and symbols, I feel, like a pulse, your spirit beating within me.*

BLESS US, LORD, as we go to worship this morning. Look upon our efforts to honor your name through song and word and fellowship. And help us do it. For only in your power do we live and move, and only in your being do we find our true identity.

❊ ❊ ❊

All I have seen teaches me to trust the
Creator for all I have not seen.

RALPH WALDO EMERSON

But the hour. . . is now here, when the true
worshipers will worship the Father in spirit
and truth, for the Father seeks such as
these to worship him. God is spirit, and
those who worship him must worship in
spirit and truth.

JOHN 4:23–24

❋   ❋   ❋

*COMING TOGETHER IN worship with prayer, song, and
psalm makes us expectant people, dear Lord. Here we find
what we came seeking: your abiding, ever-present daily
love. We leave, blessed with the truth that it goes with us
into the rest of our lives.*

❋   ❋   ❋

We have but faith: we cannot know;
For knowledge is of things we see;
And yet we trust it comes from thee,
A beam in darkness: let it grow.

ALFRED, LORD TENNYSON

WHEN I LOOK AROUND me today, may I know the blessing of seeing you, God, in every smiling face. May I reflect that blessing in my own eyes, silently with a kind heart.

In the dead of winter, God, I'm gardening.
I don't doubt the outcome because I learned at
your knee to live in faith, knowing that spring
will come. Then, with Solomon, I will rejoice:
"See! Winter is past . . . flowers appear on the
earth; the season of singing has come, the
cooing of doves is heard in the land."

How does a winter garden grow? With
hope. It grows brighter each time, because I
live knowing that you, O God, color even
our wintry days from love's spring palette.

❄   ❄   ❄

God's plans, like lilies, pure and white, unfold;
We must not tear the close-shut leaves apart;
Time will reveal the chalices of gold.

MARY LOUISE RILEY SMITH, *Sometimes*

CHAPTER 4

COMFORT
& HEALING

❈   ❈   ❈

*The Lord is my shepherd, I shall
not want. . . . your rod and your
staff—they comfort me.*

PSALM 23:1,4

This is my comfort in my distress,
that your promise gives me life.

PSALM 119:50

✳   ✳   ✳

HELD UP TO YOUR light, our broken hearts can become prisms that scatter micro-rainbows on the wall. Our pain is useless as it is, redeeming God, just as a prism is a useless chunk of glass until light passes through it. Remind us that the smallest ray of sun in a shower can create a rainbow. Use our tears as the showers and your love as the sun. Looking up, we see the tiniest arches of hope in the lightening sky.

I will turn their mourning into joy, I will comfort
them, and give them gladness for sorrow.

JEREMIAH 31:13

TIME HELPS, LORD, BUT it never quite blunts the loneliness that
loss brings. Thank you for the peace that is slowly seeping into my
being, allowing me to live with the unlivable, to bear the
unbearable. Guide and bless my faltering steps down a new road.
Prop me up when I think I can't go it alone; prod me when I
tarry too long in lonely self-pity. Most of all, Kind Healer, thank
you for the gifts of memory and dreams. The one comforts, the
other beckons, both halves of a healing whole.

We are the servants of the God of heaven
and earth, and we are rebuilding the
house that was built many years ago.

EZRA 5:11

❋　　　❋　　　❋

*L*ORD, *AS OUR WORLD reels because of countless
tragedies, I ask you in your great goodness to
hasten the healing.*

*Death and desolation have robbed us all of our
joy and innocence. Suffering has touched every
age level, from infants to the elderly.*

*Enter into every broken heart, Loving Father.
Bring mercy, compassion, and wholeness.*

*Rising out of the ashes of destruction, let the
people find a new strength and determination to
rebuild their lives.*

HELP ME TO SEE with new eyes today, especially the burden of care that others harbor within them. Grant me insight to see beyond smiling faces into hearts that hurt. And when I recognize the pain, Lord, let me reach out. Amen.

❋　　　❋　　　❋

God, promise us your comfort, and also use us as agents to comfort others. In fact, the difficulties we've gone through often give us the ability to reassure others who are now going through the same experiences. How will you use me, Lord, to extend comfort to someone else?

For thus says the Lord . . . As a mother
comforts her child, so I will comfort you.

ISAIAH 66:12–13

❇ ❇ ❇

*I DON'T BELONG to anyone now, Lord. One of my
parents died today. Who will recall the stories of my
birth? My first loose tooth? First day of school?
Who will tell me I'm special, perfect, and always
welcome no matter what? God, reach out to me, a
little child again, lost, frightened, and suddenly
orphaned. I'm no more than a marionette holding
my own strings; no one is on the other end. Stay
with me until I fall asleep and be here should I
awake, frightened. Let me be a child tonight.
Tomorrow I'll try to be strong. But for now,
Lord, find me, hold me.*

Then the Lord God said, "It is not
good that man should be alone."

GENESIS 2:18

❈   ❈   ❈

*FATHER GOD, I THANK YOU for placing people in my life to love
and to care for. All around me I see people who are lonely—so
utterly without someone to share their lives. Sometimes I think I
can almost feel their isolation.*

*Open your loving arms, Father, and envelop them with your
love. Allow them to feel your presence. Let them know that you
have the power to ease their pain and loneliness and that you can
be their friend. I pray too that you will give me the opportunity to
enter the life of someone who needs a friend.*

❈   ❈   ❈

The lonely heart withers without the
stimulation of another to share its space.

Those who sow in tears will reap with songs of joy.

PSALM 126:5 NIV

❅   ❅   ❅

AFTER A GREAT TRAGEDY, Lord, it's so hard to know how to reach
out to those who are grieving. What can I say to the parent who
loses a child? How can I comfort someone who has lost a parent?
The grief of such losses seems greater than we can bear, Lord. Yet
I know just crying with those who cry is one way to share their
burden. Thank you for healing tears, Lord. May they flow freely
and turn quickly into the joy that you promise will come.

I NEVER MEANT TO be a failure, O God of covenants and promises. I never meant to break vows solemnly made. But I am and I did. Comfort me as I mourn the truth that I could not remain in my marriage. Comfort me as I leave behind the familiar—friends, surroundings, assumptions, home, and connections. Lead me toward other friends and new landmarks, but let this new life not be created quickly and casually, Lord, as if divorce is no more serious than clipping one's fingernails. Enable me to learn something from this grieving passage so that my mistakes don't get repeated. Be with me now, Lord, as I leave not only a familiar place but also a familiar me. Grant me wisdom to go forward, toward a new home and life, solitary but free. Be with me, for the way home has never seemed longer.

But we do not want you to be uninformed, brothers and sisters, about those who have died, so that you may not grieve as others do who have no hope.

1 Thessalonians 4:13

❋   ❋   ❋

O Lord, my friend is hurting. Her whole world seems to have collapsed around her, and she fears the emptiness in her soul will consume her. Help her in her grief, Lord. Day by day, lift a bit of the heaviness from her heart. Moment by moment, fill her with your comfort. Assure her that by your grace there is hope for a future without pain and without loss. Thank you, Lord. Amen.

The Lord gave, and the Lord has taken away; blessed be the name of the Lord.

Job 1:21

❄   ❄   ❄

A FRIEND HAS JUST LOST her spouse, Lord. It is so difficult to offer her consolation. Guide me, so I do not offer meaningless phrases that add to her pain. School me in words of comfort. Grant me the sensitivity to put myself in her place and say what she needs to hear. Most of all, surround her with your love.

The Spirit of the Lord is upon me,
because . . . he hath sent me
to heal the brokenhearted.

LUKE 4:18 KJV

❊ ❊ ❊

I WISH TO EXTEND my love, Lord. Give me hands quick to work on behalf of the weak. Cause my feet to move swiftly in aid of the needy. Let my mouth speak words of encouragement and new life. And give my heart an ever-deepening joy through it all.

I will not leave you comfortless;
I will come to you.

JOHN 14:18 KJV

❅   ❅   ❅

YOU DAILY COME TO me with your solace, Heavenly Father. Now I ask that you allow me to be an instrument of your comfort. Give me opportunities to dry tears, dispense hugs, and offer cookies to your children who need reassurance. Give me words to soothe and console but also instill in me the sensitivity to know when to just keep still and listen.

❅   ❅   ❅

Healing has many faces:
The easing of tension,
The relaxing of frown lines,
The sigh of relief,
The softening in the eyes,
The quickening of the spirit,
The return of laughter.

Blessed be the God and Father of our Lord Jesus Christ, the Father of mercies and the God of all consolation, who consoles us in our affliction.

2 Corinthians 1:3–4

❄   ❄   ❄

We don't really know why we have to get sick, Lord. We only know your promise: No matter where we are or what we are called to endure, there you are in the midst of it with us, never leaving our side. Not for a split second. Thank you, Holy One.

*B*LESS THOSE WHO TEND us *when we are ailing in body, mind, and soul. They are a gift from you, Great Healer. Bless their skills, medicines, and bedside manners. Sustain them as they sustain us, for they are a channel of your love. Amen.*

❊   ❊   ❊

This seeing the sick endears them to us,
    us too it endears.
My tongue had taught thee comfort,
    touch had quenched thy tears.
        GERARD MANLEY HOPKINS, "FELIX RANDAL"

*L*ORD, SO MUCH HAS been said about the courage
and bravery of the police officers and firefighters
who work to protect us all. We do thank you for
providing them and pray for their safety. But today,
Lord, I feel especially drawn to the families of these
men and women—the wives, husbands, and children who say goodbye in the morning to the fire-
fighter or police officer they love, never knowing if
they will see them again at the end of the day. Give
these families your strength and courage, too, Lord.
Especially should the day come when they have to
make the greatest sacrifice of all. Amen.

❋   ❋   ❋

They also serve who only stand and wait.

JOHN MILTON

The Lord sustains them on their sickbed;
in their illness you heal all their infirmities.

PSALM 41:3

❋   ❋   ❋

BRING YOUR COOL caress, God, to the foreheads of
those suffering fever. By your spirit, lift the spirits of
the bedridden and give comfort to those in pain.
Strengthen all entrusted with the care of the infirm
today, and give them renewed energy for their tasks.
And remind us all that heaven awaits—where we
will all be whole and healthy before you, brothers
and sisters forever.

Her hands are so gentle and skilled,

her mind so quick,

her heart so filled with compassion.

Bless her in all her duties as a nurse,

and in her free time, too.

For she needs physical and spiritual refreshment

these days, and you, Great Physician, are the one

who can help her the best.

❊   ❊   ❊

He leadeth me O blessed thought,
O words with heavenly comfort fraught,
Whate'er I do, where'er I be,
Still 'tis God's hand that leadeth me.

JOSEPH HENRY GILMORE, "HE LEADETH ME"

O GOD, I *KNOW YOU* will never give us a burden to bear without giving us the grace to endure it, but some burdens just seem so
heavy we find ourselves wondering if they can be survived. I ask
that you fulfill your promise to send an abundant amount of
strength and grace to all those who suffer so. Let them feel your
presence in a very real way, Lord, for without you, they have no
hope. I ask this in Jesus' name. Amen.

If you could see trouble through God's eyes,
you would see God, seeing you through it.

For whatsoever things were written afore-
time were written for our learning, that we
through patience and comfort of the
scriptures might have hope.

ROMANS 15:4 KJV

❊   ❊   ❊

*M*AY I BE BLESSED *in this suffering. May I know that you can use*
this thing to show me a mistaken attitude, a destructive behavior.
In that way, may I be blessed in this suffering, O Lord, my God.

LORD, IT'S SO EASY to pray and think that you haven't heard me just because I don't see anything happening immediately! But I know that's not how you always work, Lord. You hear every prayer. It's just that sometimes you want us to wait for your answer, and sometimes your answer is "no." Teach me to pray, believing that you heard me, and to listen carefully for your answers. Amen.

❋   ❋   ❋

If you would have God hear you when you pray, you must hear Him when He speaks.

THOMAS BENTON BROOKS

O spread the tidings 'round, wherever
    man is found,
wherever human hearts and human woes
    abound;
let every Christian tongue proclaim the
    joyful sound:
The Comforter has come!

The Comforter has come, the Comforter
    has come!
The Holy Ghost from heaven,
the Father's promise given;
O spread the tidings 'round, wherever
    man is found—
the Comforter has come!

The long, long night is past, the morning
    breaks at last,
and hushed the dreadful wail and fury of
    the blast,
as over the golden hills the day advances fast!
The Comforter has come!

    Frank Bottome, "The Comforter Has Come"

Now may our Lord Jesus Christ himself and God our Father, who loved us and through grace gave us eternal comfort and good hope, comfort your hearts and strengthen them in every good work and word.

2 Thessalonians 2:16–17

❊　　❊　　❊

Someone I care about is suffering, Lord, and I feel helpless. Assure me that a little means a lot and that I'm sharing your healing love in my notes and visits. If you need me to do more, send me. I am like dandelion fluff, small but mighty in possibility. Thank you, Father.

Do not cast me off in the time of old age; do not forsake me when my strength is spent.

PSALM 70:9

❇   ❇   ❇

*L*ORD, EYES FAIL, *bones creak, and blood pressure soars, yet my mind refuses to give in to the stereotypes of old age. Help me to ignore the raised eyebrows of those who think I'm too old for new opportunities.*

Allow me, if I choose, to live out my days as if I had a lifetime still before me. I seek the comfort of your approval, Lord. The time may be short, but there is still much to accomplish.

❇   ❇   ❇

The boundaries of old age are forever moving. They are always at least 20 years older than I am.

EVERYTHING LOOKS MUCH brighter than it did before.

My prayer for strength has been answered.

My cries for help have been heard.

My pleas for mercy flew directly to your throne.

Now I'm ready to help my neighbor, Lord.

Let me not delay.

When you are in the dark, listen, and God
will give you a very precious message for
someone else when you get into the light.

OSWALD CHAMBERS

Six days you shall labor and do all your work.

Exodus 20:9

❄   ❄   ❄

AFTER MANY YEARS of faithful service, my friend has lost his job. He is stunned, Lord. His livelihood is gone. His self–esteem, sense of purpose, and enthusiasm for life have all been abruptly whisked away.

You have built in him a strong work ethic, Father. You have blessed him with a creative mind and helped him develop many talents. Yet the times have dictated that he is expendable.

He is like a revved–up motor, running in place, with no destination. Give him—and the thousands of unemployed— a sense of direction, Lord. Mend his broken spirits, and show him the road to fulfillment once again.

❄   ❄   ❄

One of life's greatest blessings is the opportunity to work at a job you enjoy and find worth doing.

See what love the Father has given us, that we should be called children of God.

1 John 3:1

❊   ❊   ❊

*L*ORD, *I* AM GLAD *to be your child. Thank you for your Holy Spirit, who watches over me. Keep me safe until you come for me, just as you promised. Amen.*

*D*EAR GOD, *HELP ME* not to take the home I have for granted. I know I'm guilty of wishing I had more space, newer carpet, or fancier furniture—when I should be on my knees by that warm, comfortable bed, thanking you for the roof over my head! Bless my home, Lord, and all who dwell within it. May I be forever grateful for the haven it is and ever mindful that it is a generous gift from you. Amen.

❊   ❊   ❊

A small house well-filled is better than an empty palace.

THOMAS D. HALIBURTON

Come to me, all you that are weary and are carrying heavy burdens, and I will give you rest. Take my yoke upon you, and learn from me; for I am gentle and humble in heart, and you will find rest for your souls. For my yoke is easy, and my burden is light.

MATTHEW 11:28–30

❋   ❋   ❋

MAY I BE HEALED, in mind, body, and soul. May I come to know that all healing proceeds from you, God, and you care about every part of me. Perhaps the healing will come sooner for my attitude than for my body. Perhaps my mind will experience peace quicker than bones and muscles. But sooner or later, all will be well.

For my thoughts are not your thoughts,
nor are your ways my ways, says the Lord.

ISAIAH 55:8

*G*OD, *IT'S SO HARD* to see your will in suffering. But
while I can't understand your ways, Lord, I trust your
heart. And so I cling to the faith that has sustained me
through so many heartaches before, knowing that
although it may be all I have, it's also all I need. Amen.

He said to them, " . . . For truly I tell you, if you have faith the size of a mustard seed, you will say to this mountain, 'Move from here to there,' and it will move; and nothing will be impossible for you."

MATTHEW 17:20–21

❊ ❊ ❊

O GOD, HEALING IS going so-o-o slowly, and I am impatient and grumpy. Mind, body, or soul, this could take a long time. Remind me that recovery is a journey, not a hasty jet-lagged arrival. Bless me with faith to sustain me, step by small step. You do miraculous things with faith as tiny as mustard seeds that, in time, blossom into awesome growth. I hold that picture as I make mustard-seed progress along the road to healing.

A cheerful heart is a good medicine,
but a downcast spirit dries up the bones.

PROVERBS 17:22

❋   ❋   ❋

A SICKROOM IS OFTEN a somber place, Lord.
When I visit the seriously ill, I am tempted to put
on my sober face and commiserate with the patient.

But, Father, you remind me that cheerfulness is
good medicine.

Instill in me the gifts of humor and joy. Teach me
how to lift downcast spirits and dispense the medi-
cine of good cheer in your name.

❋   ❋   ❋

Humor is proof of man's ability to overcome adversity.

WHEN WE DOUBT your miracle-making power, Lord, show us the ordinary miracles of seasons, of hope regained, of love from family and friends, and of surprises that turn out miraculous simply by remaking our lives.

❋　　❋　　❋

The little cares that fretted me,
I lost them yesterday,
Among the fields above the sea,
Among the winds at play, . . .
Among the husking of the corn,
Where drowsy poppies nod,
Where ill thoughts die and good are born—
Out in the fields with God.

ELIZABETH BARRETT BROWNING
AND LOUISE IMOGEN GUINEY
"OUT IN THE FIELDS WITH GOD"

"I am the Alpha and the Omega," says the Lord God, who is and who was and who is to come, the Almighty.

REVELATION 1:8

✳   ✳   ✳

O GOD, YOU TELL us you are the Alpha and the Omega, the beginning and the end. As this is true for eternity, may it be true within the limited confines of each day. I want to begin each day in prayer to you, Lord, and end each day with a heart full of gratitude. Please be my Alpha and Omega today and every day, even throughout eternity. Amen.

On the day I called, you answered me,
you increased my strength of soul.

PSALM 138:3

❊ ❊ ❊

God hears my cries for help,
and He answers every prayer.
I only need be patient—
He supplies the "how" and "where."

Sometimes it may be immediate
In a tangible way I'll know;
While other times I wait assured
That He is strengthening my soul.

His grace is all-sufficient
To meet my heart-cries need.
As I lean upon His promises,
Walking in faith, He'll lead.

Thank you, Lord, for reddened eyes. Believing your promise that comfort follows mourning, we bawl and sob. We're grateful for these healing tears. Amen.

The Comforting Spirit shows you what it means
to let go the hope that others will be the cure.
The Great Physician will be your healer in this
quiet hour.

*MAY MY THOUGHTS focus much more upon what
I have than what I lack in this trying time.*

*May my heart lay hold of present realities rather
than future possibilities.*

For this moment—the now—is all I am given.

*Whether I am sick or healthy, this juncture in time
is the place I share with you.*

*Let me be blessed in this moment, needing nothing
to change. Let me simply be in your presence,
God, just for this moment.*

❊   ❊   ❊

In the midst of mourning life's troubles,
you come to us.
In the darkness, your spirit moves, spreading light like a shower of stars against a
stormy night sky.

It is not enemies who taunt me—I could bear that; it is not adversaries who deal insolently with me—I could hide from them. But it is you, my equal, my companion, my familiar friend, with whom I kept pleasant company.

Psalm 55:12–14

❅   ❅   ❅

My friend and I have had a falling-out, Lord. The atmosphere is strained between us; the air is chilly. I don't know what I've said or done to cause this breach in our relationship. I only know we're both at odds. Relieve the anguish that I feel, Lord. Show me how to break the silence. Help me to take the first step to mend this rift between us, then you can do the rest. Heal us with your love.

❅   ❅   ❅

Hold on tight to your friends; they are God's great blessings.

Abide in me as I abide in you.

John 15:4

❋   ❋   ❋

Abide with me,
Fast falls the eventide;
The darkness deepens;
Lord, with me abide!
When other helpers fail
And comforts flee,
Help of the helpless,
O abide with me.

I need thy presence
Every passing hour;
What but thy grace
Can foil the tempter's power?
Who, like thyself,
My guide and stay can be?
Through cloud and sunshine,
Lord, abide with me.

Henry F. Lyte, "Abide With Me"

I have loved you with an everlasting
love; therefore I have continued
my faithfulness to you.

Jeremiah 31:3

✳ ✳ ✳

I NEED YOUR COMFORT, God.

I need to feel your strong arms embracing me.

I don't need wise words or brilliant truth—just be there
for me now.

Remind me of your love for me. Tell me everything's going
to be all right.

Assure me again that you know what I'm going through,
because you've been there.

You have felt my pain, and now you can share it.

Thank you for sitting with me through this crisis.

I praise you for your awesome love.

Then your light shall break forth like the
dawn, and your healing shall spring up
quickly.

Isaiah 58:8

❊   ❊   ❊

Finally, I've emerged from the dark night

into the light with new energy,

renewed vigor, a body that responds again.

Thank you for recovery and wholeness.

And bless me as I tell others how good you are! Amen.

❊   ❊   ❊

O God, our help in ages past,
Our hope for years to come;
Be Thou our guide while life shall last,
And our eternal home.
Isaac Watts, "O God, Our Help in Ages Past"

> But for you who fear my name, the Sun of
> Righteousness will rise with healing in his
> wings. And you will go free...
>
> Malachi 4:2 NLT

❊　　　❊　　　❊

The chains that have bound me are flung to the wind,
by the mercy of God the poor slave is set free.
And the strong arm of heaven breathes fresh
    o'er the mind,
like the bright winds of summer that brighten the sea.

I cried out in mercy, and fell on my knees,
and confessed, while my heart with keen
    sorrow was wrung;
'twas the labor of minutes, and years of disease
fell as fast from my soul as the words from my tongue.

And now, blest be God and the sweet Lord who died!
No deer on the mountain, no bird in the sky,
no dark wave that leaps on the dark bounding tide,
is a creature so free or so happy as I.

Frederick William Farber, "A Good Confession"

Jesus said to him, "Go; your son will live."
The man believed the word that Jesus
spoke to him and started on his way.

JOHN 4:50

❄   ❄   ❄

*F*ATHER, *OF ALL THE* emergencies in my life, the
illness of a child—my child—is the one I dread most.
I can't bear to see my little one in pain. My mind
works overtime imagining all that could go wrong.
I fret and stew as my anxieties overwhelm me.

Please be with my child today. Bring your soothing
comfort. Heal him, Lord; then heal me.

❄   ❄   ❄

Pray your prayers, then stand
back and watch God work.

MENTAL ILLNESS CAN be so devastating, Lord. Few understand the heartaches involved in diseases that carry no apparent physical scars.

Be with those friends, neighbors, and family members who deal daily with difficult situations of which we are often unaware. Touch them with your special love, and let them know that they can lean on you, Lord.

Ease their burdens, quell their sadness, calm their desperation. Bring peace and healing to these households.

❄   ❄   ❄

Mental illness is a thief, robbing
the mind of its pleasures and reason.

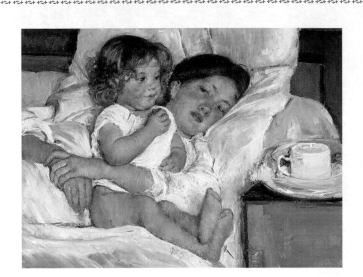

Daughter, your faith has made you
well; go in peace, and be healed.

Mark 5:34

❄   ❄   ❄

*L*ORD, WHEN I'M NOT *feeling well it's so hard for me to reach*
out to other people. All I want to do is curl up in bed with the
covers over my head! But I want to be active again, Lord, and I
need to care for my family. Please wrap your healing arms around
me and restore my health and energy. Thank you, Lord. Amen.

He got up, rebuked the wind and said to the waves, "Quiet! Be still!" Then the wind died down and it was completely calm.

Mark 4:39 NIV

❄   ❄   ❄

Father God, we ask for your protection from the storms of life. Like rainstorms, the storms that befall us sometimes build for a while. Other times, they hit suddenly. But you, O God, are the Creator and the calmer of the storm. May we learn to be grateful both for the storm that rages and for the One who has it under control. Amen.

I KNOW IN MY HEART I have to walk alongside a friend who is hurting, Lord. It isn't enough just to send flowers and a card saying, "I'll pray for you." As helpless as I feel in the face of grief and confusion, please give me the courage to be there. I can't dry the flowing tears or answer the agonizing questions, Lord, but you can. If I faithfully walk beside my friend, you will be walking with us. Then there will be hope, healing, and renewed joy! Thank you for this wonderful promise of comfort, Lord.

LORD, I KNOW YOU recognize that every life we lose is a gift to be treasured, a loss to be mourned, and a part of our hearts forever. Thank you for understanding that although we believe in eternal life, it hurts so much to lose someone we love. Comfort those who are grieving, Lord. Fill them with the knowledge that you are grieving with them and will carry them through this difficult time.

❊   ❊   ❊

When someone we love dies, God hides a smile in every memory and hope in every tear.

I SEE SO MANY PEOPLE walking through this life completely void of hope. There is no light in their eyes, Lord. They are so beaten down by life that they can barely get out of bed in the morning, let alone face the day with a bounce in their steps. Lord, I pray that you would touch these lost souls, these weary hearts, with the glorious truth of your love for them. Give them that blessed assurance, that hope, that only comes from trusting in you. For it is the hope you give us that makes all our days worth living. In your name I pray, amen.

�֍   ✤   ✤

We have high hopes because
our hope comes from on high.

I will . . . lie down and sleep in peace; for you alone, O Lord, make me lie down in safety.

Psalm 4:8

❊   ❊   ❊

Lord, how i love to crawl into bed at the end of the day knowing that, for that day at least, my work is done. Thank you for creating sleep to heal and comfort us. How often something that was a big concern one day looks far more manageable in the morning because I bathed it in prayer, turned off the light, and went to sleep. I know sleep is a gift from you, Lord. Thank you for giving me perfect rest in you. Amen.

Pray for one another, so that you may be healed.

JAMES 5:16

❋   ❋   ❋

I HAVE ALWAYS FELT *prayer to be a very personal and individual matter. Each day I pray faithfully and feverishly for my loved ones and others who need my prayers.*

But in your great goodness, God, you have shown me the power of friends praying together. It has been a profound and comforting experience to pray with others and to be named aloud in prayer by someone I care about.

Thank you, Lord, for the faithful friends you have sent to pray, not just for me, but with me.

My child, if you accept my words and treasure
up my commandments within you . . . then you
will understand the fear of the Lord and find
the knowledge of understanding.

PROVERBS 2:1,5

❄   ❄   ❄

Today may you come to acceptance.
What is, is.
May you find blessed relief in seeing—
    without judging,
being—without having to become,
knowing—without needing to change
    a thing.
Then, should you be healed, it will be a
    gracious, unexpected surprise.
May you soon arrive at perfect acceptance.

When peace, like a river, attends my way,
when sorrows like sea billows roll;
whatever my lot, you have taught me to say,
"It is well, it is well with my soul."

Though Satan should buffet, though trials
    should come,
let this blest assurance control,
that Christ has regarded my helpless estate,
and has shed his own blood for my soul.

My sin—O the bliss of this glorious
    thought—
my sin, not in part, but the whole,
is nailed to the cross, and I bear it no more,
praise the Lord, praise the Lord, O my soul!

And, Lord, haste the day when my faith
    shall be sight,
the clouds be rolled back as a scroll,
the trumpet shall sound and the Lord shall
    descend,
even so—it is well with my soul.

HORATIO G. SPAFFORD, "IT IS WELL WITH MY SOUL"

CHAPTER 5

FORGIVENESS

❄   ❄   ❄

Be kind to one another,
tenderhearted, forgiving one
another, as God . . . has
forgiven you.

EPHESIANS 4:32

Bear with one another and, if anyone
has a complaint against another, forgive
each other; just as the Lord has forgiven
you, so you also must forgive.

Colossians 3:13

❇   ❇   ❇

*L*ORD GOD, THE WORDS *"I'm sorry"* and *"forgive me"* have got
*to be among the most powerful in our vocabulary. May these
phrases ever be poised at my lips, ready to do their work of release
and restoration. I need to forgive, and I need to be forgiven. Let
your healing balm wash over me, Father, as I both grant and
receive the freedom that forgiveness brings.*

❇   ❇   ❇

To be forgiven is to be absolved of all
charges of guilt and responsibility. To
forgive is more freeing still. It is release
from a prison of your own making.

I will forgive their iniquity, and
remember their sin no more.

JEREMIAH 31:34

❊   ❊   ❊

*Y*OUR MODEL OF FORGIVENESS *is my inspiration, Merciful God.
If you, our Creator, can overlook humankind's shortcomings,
how can I do less? You are a God of second chances. You have
demonstrated your compassion since the world began.*

*Build up in me, Lord, the same will to rid myself of anger and to
forget grievances both large and small against friends and loved
ones. Help me to understand that when I forgive I am not deny-
ing my right to be angry. I am merely acknowledging that right,
then moving on, releasing myself from the emotional burden.
Thank you, Lord, for this great gift.*

❊   ❊   ❊

Forgiveness is the medicine that heals the world.

Keep your tongue from evil, and
your lips from speaking deceit.

PSALM 34:13

✻   ✻   ✻

I CONFESS, LORD, that I did something I shouldn't have done. I criticized a friend behind her back. Now word has gotten back to her and she is hurt. You have warned your children about misusing the tongue. I know better, but the words just slipped out.

I'm not sure if it's possible to repair our relationship, but please help me to find the right time and place to ask her forgiveness. I ask your forgiveness, too, Father, for disappointing you and for failing to speak in love. Amen.

Come, let us go up to the mountain of
the Lord . . . that he may teach us his
ways and that we may walk in his paths.

Isaiah 2:3

❋ ❋ ❋

You are a God of forgiveness, and you gave me a gift, Heavenly Father, when you taught me how to forgive. Now, with your help, I want to teach my children the importance of forgiveness. I want them to know how letting go of anger and other negative emotions can be a release for them as well as for the person forgiven. Help me to teach them at an early age, Lord, so they can learn the habit of forgiving quickly, before resentment is allowed to fester. And please help me foster in our home a climate in which they can learn to forgive themselves.

Lord, speak to me through these pages.
Let me hear your gentle words
Come whispering through the ages
And thundering through the world.

Challenge me and change me,
Comfort me and calm.
Completely rearrange me,
Soothe me with a psalm.

Teach me how to please you,
Show me how to live.
Inspire me to praise you
For all the love you give.

If we confess our sins, he who is faithful
and just will forgive us our sins and
cleanse us from all unrighteousness.

1 John 1:9

❄   ❄   ❄

*WHAT A DEAL, LORD! You mean all I have to do
is confess my wrongdoings, and the slate is wiped
clean? It can't get any better than that. But wait.
Didn't you have to make a huge sacrifice for this
privilege? You say I'm worth it? I am your child,
and you love me? Thank you, Father. I love you,
too, and I accept your offer—gladly!*

❄   ❄   ❄

Admitting our guilt is like taking a
warm shower and washing away all
the grime and dirt that has clung
to us all day. We feel clean again!

Forgive, and you will be forgiven.

Luke 6:37

❊   ❊   ❊

*W*HEN WE FAIL TO FORGIVE, *Father, we think we are punishing the other person with our hate, but we are the ones who suffer most. Fill us with your wisdom, Father. Teach us to rid ourselves of the crippling emotions of hate, resentment, and revenge, and replace them with your love. Amen.*

"Lord, if another member of the church sins against me, how often should I forgive? As many as seven times?" Jesus said to him, "Not seven times, but, I tell you, seventy-seven times."

MATTHEW 18:21

❋　　　❋　　　❋

LORD, MY MOM IS VERY accepting of others' faults. Rather than criticizing, she continually looks for reasons for a person's undesirable behavior. You've shown me that in doing so she is practicing a form of forgiveness, even though the individual's behavior may have nothing to do with her. Thank you for her great example to me, Lord. Help me to be more like her, to look beyond surface behavior to the underlying causes, and to pardon.

❋　　　❋　　　❋

We should be willing to pardon others as many times as we pardon ourselves.

For if you forgive others their trespasses,
your heavenly Father will also forgive you;
but if you do not forgive others, neither
will your Father forgive your trespasses.

MATTHEW 6:14

❄   ❄   ❄

*I NEED FOR YOU to help me, Lord, with the concept
of forgiving people over and over again for the same
behavior. I know you taught that there was no limit
to the number of times we should forgive someone,
but I get so weary of doing it, Lord. Help me have a
heart of forgiveness, so ready to forgive that I do so
before the person who has wronged me even seeks
my forgiveness. There's freedom in that kind of
forgiveness, Lord. Help me claim it for my own.*

❄   ❄   ❄

Let us be quick to forgive so
that we may be quickly forgiven.

Should you not have mercy on your fellow slave as I had mercy on you?

MATTHEW 18:33

❊   ❊   ❊

THANK YOU FOR your parable of the unforgiving servant, Lord. It is a reminder of our debt to you and to society: to pass on the blessings we have received.

When someone cancels a debt I owe, they have a right to expect that, out of gratitude, I will "pay it forward," passing on my good fortune to another. Help me to be faithful to this principle, Father, and to put in motion a chain of forgiveness that could reach around the world. Amen.

All who hate a brother or sister are murderers.

1 John 3:5

*F*ATHER OF MERCY, *I am amazed at your generosity. You contin-*
ually find goodness in me, Lord, even when I am at my worst.
You bless me, even though I have sinned. You remind us that all
those who hate are murderers, that without love we are dead,
and that those who refuse to help another are not your children.

Am I missing something here, Lord? Teach me your loving-kindness
and your mercy, so you won't find me guilty of hating others.

He has said, "I will never leave you or forsake you." So we can say with confidence, "The Lord is my helper; I will not be afraid."

Hebrews 13:5–6

❋   ❋   ❋

I ASK YOU TO comfort those who feel abandoned, Father. Help them understand you will never fail or forsake them. Lead them down the path of acceptance, so forgiveness is possible and life can go on. Amen.

❋   ❋   ❋

God does not leave you comfortless. He provides you a shoulder to lean on and the soothing words of friends to ease your sorrow.

When I find myself being caught up by the
   desire to acquire,
Change my heart, O God.
When I feel disappointed in people in my
   family or at work,
Change my heart, O God.
When unreal expectations send me spiral-
   ing into dark depression,
Change my heart, O God.
When I hesitate to do those acts of kind-
   ness so pleasing to you,
Change my heart, O God.
When I cling to the need to have my own
   way in every situation,
Change my heart, O God.
When I give in to the temptation to com-
   pare myself to others,
Change my heart, O God.
For it's only through your forgiveness, and
   with a heart renewed by your hand, that
   I can know contentment.

Create in me a clean heart, O God, and
put a new and right spirit within me.

PSALM 51:10

❊   ❊   ❊

LORD, YOU PROMISE *that when we ask for forgiveness you not only forgive us but also vow to
remember our sin no more. You say our sin is
buried deep in the sea, so if it comes to mind it's
because we somehow managed to dredge it up
again. The only reason we should remember past
sins at all is to keep from repeating them or so we
can proclaim your mercy. Free me from the guilt
of past sins, Lord, and forgive all my present sins—
sins of omission and commission. Thank you for
your amazing grace! For when you forgive us,
we are forgiven indeed. Amen.*

This is the day that the Lord has made;
let us rejoice and be glad in it.

Psalm 118:24

❋ ❋ ❋

*F*ATHER, I NEED TO ASK *for your forgiveness today. Instead of waking with a joyful spirit, I let all the things I have to do make me quick to complain and slow to praise you. Yet I know each day I live is a precious gift from you—one not to be put on a shelf and ignored but to be opened and enjoyed! Forgive me for failing to accept your gift graciously today, Lord. I do thank you for it with all my heart.*

I COME TO YOU, Lord, with a heavy and contrite heart. I know that what I did was wrong and, of course, so do you. Please forgive my foolish ways, Lord. Help me swallow my pride and give me the courage to say "I'm sorry" and mean it. Please go before me to prepare the way so that my apology will be heard and accepted. In your name I pray, amen.

❄   ❄   ❄

Being sorry is the beginning of being forgiven. Being forgiven is the beginning of being free.

*L*ORD, MAKE ME *whole.*

Like the woman who touched your cloak for healing,

I reach out to you, O Lord.

Hoping, believing, trusting, longing for your power.

I don't want to be some otherworldly pious person.

I don't need other people to say "There goes someone holy!"

I just want to please you with my life.

Fill me with your fullness.

Make me all you created me to be.

Amen.

But those who wait for the Lord shall renew their strength, they shall mount up with wings like eagles, they shall run and not be weary, they shall walk and not faint.

Isaiah 40:31

❋   ❋   ❋

We live in a world where waiting is seen as an empty, useless waste of time, Lord. It's difficult for us to learn to wait productively in a society where waiting is seen as passive. But those who wait on the Lord wait actively, tirelessly, hopefully, and triumphantly! So often it takes time for us to see what you are doing in our lives—and it all unfolds in your time, not ours. Forgive my impatience, Lord. For I know that waiting for you is never a waste of time.

GOD, GUIDE ME in small decisions and insignificant choices. I know the smallest act on my part can have ramifications that will either bring glory to your name or cause others to turn away from you. And the things that seem small and insignificant to me may not be so in the light of your kingdom. Forgive my shortsightedness, Lord. Give me the eyes to see everyday opportunities the way you see them. Make me wise in little ways. Amen.

❋　　　❋　　　❋

It seems so insignificant,
this choice you have to make.
Yet the Lord can use small acts of faith
to cause the earth to shake!
So pray and wait to know his will
for decisions made today,
and the Lord may use your faithfulness
to show someone the way.

*F*ORGIVE ME FOR *falling into the trap of comparing myself to others, Lord. When I notice how I am different from them in terms of appearance or abilities I can get discouraged. But you don't see our differences, do you, Lord? While I'm busy looking at the outward appearances of those I see, you are looking only at their hearts. Teach me to see differences as you do, Lord, as beautiful variations in your creation, not as mistakes or disabilities. I ask that you make me blind to differences in the color of skin, length of hair—anything that sets us apart from one another. Thank you for the knowledge that in your eyes we are all beautiful, all deserving of your grace and mercy.*

❅ ❅ ❅

Red and yellow, black and white,
They are precious in His sight.
REV. C. H. WOOLSTON

Lord, so often I find myself praying for something when I should really be praying with something—with my hands full of all the useless worries, heartaches, and failures that clutter my life. Teach me to lay them all at your feet, Lord, that I may be free of them forever! Amen.

❄   ❄   ❄

Give the Lord your worries,
and then let him keep them.

*I WONDER HOW MANY times I've had the oppor-
tunity to tell someone else what you've done in my
life, Lord, only to walk away without saying a
word. You see, Lord, in order to get to the part of
the story where you saved me from my sins, it's
necessary for me to confess the sins to someone new.
My shame or my pride, perhaps both, makes it
difficult for me to do that sometimes, Lord. Yet I
know that I must never be ashamed of your saving
grace, and that by sharing what you've done for
me I might be encouraging someone else to turn to
you. So forgive my hesitation, Lord.*

❄   ❄   ❄

I pray that until the day I die I will be able to tell
all the people I meet what you have done for me.

Bless the Lord, O my soul, and do not forget all his benefits—who forgives all your iniquity, who heals all your diseases.

Psalm 103:2–3

❋ ❋ ❋

Lord, I confess to you,
sadly, my sin;
all I am, I tell to you,
all I have been.
Purge all my sin away,
wash clean my soul this day;
Lord, make me clean.

Then all is peace and
light this soul within;
thus shall I walk with you,
loved though unseen.
Leaning on you, my God,
guided along the road,
nothing between!

Horatius Bonar

As HARD AS WE may try, God, there are times when we will make human mistakes. Even so, if we trust in you and ask your forgiveness, you will bless us with mercy and peace. Lord, I'm glad you are merciful and gracious. Today I'm resting in your steadfast love and in your hugs. Amen.

❄   ❄   ❄

O most merciful Redeemer,
    friend, and brother;
may we know Thee more clearly,
    love Thee more dearly,
and follow Thee more nearly,
    day by day.

RICHARD OF CHICHESTER

FORGIVE US, LORD, our sins, for failing to live up to your standards of goodness and justice. We confess our shortcomings. Make us willing to change and help us become persons of godly character.

❋   ❋   ❋

The Lord hath spoken peace to my soul,
He hath blessed me abundantly,
Hath pardoned my sins;
He hath shown me great mercy
   and saved me by his love.
I will sing of his goodness and mercy while I live,
And ever, forever will praise his holy name.
O how sweet to trust in God,
And to know your sins forgiven,
To believe his precious word,
And be guided by his love.
Therefore goodness and mercy,
Shall follow me all the days of my life.
Amen.

C. E. LESLIE, *Leslie's Crown of Song*

I acknowledged my sin unto thee, and
mine iniquity have I not hid. I said, I will
confess my transgressions unto the Lord;
and thou forgavest the iniquity of my sin.

PSALM 32:5 KJV

❋   ❋   ❋

*MANY TIMES, LORD, I may come to the place where it is difficult
to "feel" forgiven. But I know that is where faith comes in. And
the very basis of faith is the belief in you that you cannot lie.*

❋   ❋   ❋

No, but I'm as sure
As there's a God in Heaven.
For feelings come, and feelings go,
And feelings are deceiving.
My warrant is the Word of God,
Naught else is worth believing.

MARTIN LUTHER, ON WHETHER HE FELT FORGIVEN

Our sins are forgiven by God's mercy
alone. We can't earn forgiveness by forgiving others. But when we withhold forgiveness from others after having received it
ourselves, it shows we don't understand or
appreciate God's mercy toward us.

James 2:13 TLB

*God, when we receive your forgiveness, I know we
should pass it on freely to others. I pray for the grace
of insight to look within myself and see the part I may
have played in this troubling event and to see if the
other person was carrying some wound. Help me to
dissolve my anger and understand, not look for
excuses or assign blame. I know I must acknowledge
the trouble in order for healing to begin.*

Now is the time to forgive this man
and help him back on his feet. If all
you do is pour on the guilt, you
could very well drown him in it. My
counsel now is to pour on the love.
    2 Corinthians 2:7 *The Message*

❊   ❊   ❊

I NEED TO UNDERSTAND, Lord, that forgiveness is not
dependent on my feelings but rather on a determination
of my will. Help me to form a few well-chosen words
of forgiveness that will act like an antiseptic and
cleanse the wound to bring about healing. Amen.

❊   ❊   ❊

Pray you now, forget and forgive.
    William Shakespeare, *King Lear*

Lord, give me words.

I never know what to say.

Lord, give me wisdom.

I never know when to say it.

Lord, give me love

that I won't say it rudely.

Lord, give me faith

that you'll make the best of my feeble efforts.

Lord, give me passion

to care for those who need to know you.

Lord, give me vision

to see what they could become.

Lord, give me ears

to hear what they are really asking.

Lord, give me words

to share my love for you.

SOMETIMES IT SEEMS impossible to forgive other people, dear God, especially if they are purposely trying to hurt me. But I remind myself that if Jesus could forgive the people who crucified him, then I should be able to forgive those who have hurt me. Amen.

When on the fragrant sandal-tree
The woodman's axe descends,
And she who bloomed so beauteously
Beneath the keen stroke bends,
E'en on the edge that wrought her death
Dying she breathed her sweetest breath,
As if to token, in her fall,
Peace to her foes, and love to all.

How hardly man this lesson learns,
To smile and bless the hand that spurns;
To see the blow, to feel the pain,
But render only love again!
This spirit not to earth is given—
One had it, but he came from heaven.
Reviled, rejected, and betrayed,
No curse he breathed, no plaint he made,
But when in death's deep pain he sighed
Prayed for his murderers, and died.

AUTHOR UNKNOWN

FORGIVENESS DEMANDS we get in touch with our anger and bitterness—and get past the denial of built-up resentments. We cannot be bitter and be led by you, God, at the same time. Unconsciously we may say, "I choose to react toward them with bitterness." We choose our attitude in any circumstance. Unfortunately, we seldom vent our anger at the intended person, but rather our family members and friends must bear the brunt of our outbursts.

Forgiveness is not always possible on our own. That's when we must pray to you, God: In my own strength, it is impossible for me to forgive. I am ready to be made willing to forgive this person. Help me find the strength to make the phone call or write the letter that will begin the healing process.

Do not repay anyone evil for evil. Be careful to do what is right in the eyes of everybody. If it is possible, as far as it depends on you, live at peace with everyone. Do not take revenge, my friends, but leave room for God's wrath, for it is written: "It is mine to avenge; I will repay," says the Lord.

ROMANS 12:17–19 NIV

❊ ❊ ❊

TOTAL FORGIVENESS MEANS first I ask you, God, for forgiveness of my poor attitude and for your help. Then I must go to the other party and ask their forgiveness. And as I ask, I must be ready and willing to offer forgiveness.

It is only as I thank you, God, for your forgiveness that I sense my anger and bitterness slipping away, and I am able to get on with the process of living.

GOD IN HEAVEN, you teach us that even if we feel we've been wronged by someone, if we soften our hearts and forgive the one who wronged us, the burden of bitterness will be lifted. Help me to forgive and shed my crippling burden of hurt. By making this change in my attitude, I am certain to affect the lives of those around me. Amen.

❈   ❈   ❈

An apology is a friendship preserver, an antidote for hatred, never a sign of weakness; it costs nothing but one's pride, always saves more than it costs, and is a device needed in every home.

AUTHOR UNKNOWN

*W*E'RE STAINED, LIKE *a paint rag, by troubles we caused ourselves, Lord.*

Red, the color of lost temper and rudeness.
Green, envy of others who have it easier and more of it.
Blue, the shade of despair over something we could change.
Yellow, of cowardly running.

Rearrange our unsightly smudges into glorious rainbows through your gift of forgiveness. Amen.

LORD, WE KNOW that revenge will settle nothing at this point. It will only leave us with an emptier feeling than before. Heal the pain in our hurts over this injustice, and somehow, as impossible as it now seems, bring us to the place of blessing our enemies and extending the one thing that keeps saving our own lives: your forgiveness.

❅   ❅   ❅

God pardons like a mother who kisses the offense into everlasting forgetfulness.

HENRY WARD BEECHER

LET ME KNOW the tranquility of forgiving today, O Lord.

I have held my peace, doused my anger.

Now it is time to extend my hand. Amen.

He that cannot forgive others, breaks the bridge over which he himself must pass if he would ever reach heaven, for everyone has need to be forgiven.

GEORGE HERBERT

*G*OD OF EASTER SURPRISES, *bring back to life friendships faded because of hurt feelings, marriages broken from deceit, love crushed by meanness. In the doing, hope glimmers like dawn's first sun ray and thaws even the most frozen heart.*

❄   ❄   ❄

One word frees us of all the weight
and pain in life. That word is love.

SOPHOCLES

*P*RAISE WELLS UP *within my soul, dear God, when I consider the friends you have placed in my life along the way. We can know the pleasure of conversation, laughter, tears, encouragement, honesty, and love within the context of friendship.*

It is true that sometimes we have our differences, but forgiveness and under-standing have healed and held our hearts together. And as we walk arm in arm through whatever lies ahead, good or bad, I will remember to praise you for these friends who make my journey a more joyful experience.

E<small>NTER AND BLESS</small> *this family, Lord, so that its circle will be where quarrels are resolved and relationships mature; where failures are forgiven and new directions are found. Amen.*

Dear Lord and Father of humankind,
Forgive our foolish ways;
Reclothe us in our rightful mind,
In purer lives Thy service find,
In deeper reverence, praise.

<small>JOHN GREENLEAF WHITTIER</small>, *The Brewing of Soma*

For you, O Lord, are good and
forgiving, abounding in steadfast love to all who call on you.

PSALM 86:5

❈　　❈　　❈

HEAL THE DIFFERENCES between me
and my spouse, Lord. We argued and
then let the sun go down on our anger.
We said things that we can't take back,
and shameful words were spoken.
Please give me the grace to ask for
forgiveness and to offer forgiveness.
I ask this in the name of Jesus, amen.

*L*ORD, TEACH ME *how to let go.*

I cling to my pain and curse those who caused it.

  Show me the joy of forgiveness.

I cling to my pride and refuse to change long-held ways.

  Show me the delight of singing new songs.

I cling to my worries and imprison myself in fear.

  Show me the freedom of trusting you.

Lord, teach me how to let go of all this so I can embrace you.

You are a God ready to forgive,
gracious and merciful, slow to anger
and abounding in steadfast love.

NEHEMIAH 9:17

✻ ✻ ✻

IT'S HARD FOR ME to come to you when I've made such a mess of things. But I know that you are the only one to whom I can turn. Examine my heart, Lord, and you will see how sorry I am for the mistakes I've made. I ask for your forgiveness first of all. I also ask that you would give me your insight into how I can make the best of this situation.

Rescue me through your mercy, Lord. Amen.

*L*ORD, MAY WE TAKE *a moment and concentrate on*
forgiveness. Grant me a forgiving spirit, one that fits
with your expectations and commandments. Help me to
give up hidden resentments, foolish ill will, and time-
wasting thoughts of other souls along their own paths.
Forgiveness does not come naturally to me. But I pray
that you will abide with me awhile, so that when I get off
my knees, the weight of my unforgiving spirit will lift from
my shoulders. Lord, I want to be able to stand before
you, forgiven of my own sins, and so I must do the same
on earth. Bear with me, stay with me, give me grace.

MY HEART IS HEAVY, God. I realize now at the end of the day that I haven't thought of you once. I haven't considered how you would want me to act, whether you had something for me to do, or if anything I did was simply against your Word.

It's so silly. I know I can't do this on my own, yet today I took on the whole world as though I'm the only person who counts. Please forgive me.

Help me not to slide so far into my own plans that I forget your timetable is far more important than anything I could come up with. Again, forgive me, and let me be always mindful of your presence in my life.

Some take pride in chariots, and some in horses,
but our pride is in the name of the Lord our God.

PSALM 20:7

*P*RIDE GOT THE BETTER *of me today, Lord. You helped me to
prepare, you granted me peace, you gave me courage. And I
took all the credit. So, here I am, asking even more from you:
Please forgive me so that I can get up off my knees as a
forgiven person. I ask it in your holy name. Amen.*

I will cleanse them from all the guilt of their sin against me, and I will forgive all the guilt of their sin and rebellion against me.

JEREMIAH 33:8

❋   ❋   ❋

I'VE HAD THE RUG pulled out from under my feet, Lord. As I pray, fill me with your wonderful grace. Help me to accept this new challenge with calm, forgiveness, understanding, and trust in your purpose for my life. Amen.

❋   ❋   ❋

The greater part of our happiness depends on our disposition and not our circumstances.

MARTHA WASHINGTON

WE COME, *NEEDING your help to move beyond the times we hurt one another, the times we willingly misunderstand, cherishing our differences, and the times we assume we know all there is to know about each other and turn away.*

Then there are the times when we make private rules, only to publicly condemn anyone who fails to abide by them. We limit one another by labeling, interpreting, conditioning, insisting, resisting, defining.

From all this, Lord, we come, asking that you forgive us as we forgive those others. We need new eyes to see and new ears to hear. Be with us as we do so.

Those who despise their neighbors are
sinners.

PROVERBS 14:21

❋   ❋   ❋

*P*ROMINENT CHURCH *leader Desmond Tutu has said that without*
forgiveness we have no future. Lord, when I think of situations in
the world where revenge is a religion, I shudder. I envision the
self-destruction of entire nations that ignore your basic law of
love and withhold their forgiveness.

Please awaken in these nations the understanding of the need to
forgive their enemies who are their neighbors. Instill in all of us
the knowledge that forgiveness is not just an ideal but a necessity
for survival, an assurance of our future.

❋   ❋   ❋

Sometimes to give in is to win.

You are the light of the world. A city built on a hill cannot be hid. No one after lighting a lamp puts it under the bushel basket, but on the lampstand, and it gives light to all in the house. In the same way, let your light shine before others, so that they may see your good works and give glory to your Father in heaven.

Matthew 5:14–16

❋   ❋   ❋

Bless this country and those whom you have chosen to lead it, God. So often we fear for the future of this land we love. We see the scars of violence and the heartbreak of those who are left in its wake. We see corruption, and we pray for your forgiveness. Please bless us all with your wisdom and discernment, God. Turn the hearts of this country back to you that we might become all you intended for us to be—a light in the world you created.

If a shepherd has a hundred sheep, and
one of them has gone astray, does he not
leave the ninety-nine on the mountains
and go in search of the one that went
astray? . . . It is not the will of your Father
in heaven that one of these little ones
should be lost.

MATTHEW 18:12, 14

❊   ❊   ❊

*THE HARDEST PART of forgiveness, Father, is decid-
ing to forgive. It does not make sense, for I want to
settle a score with the ill-doer. Reconciliation does
not seem possible now. But I know that my holding
on to the resentment and anger traps me in the past.
Help me let go and forgive, God, so I may be free
from dwelling in painful memories, free to move
on—free to come home to you. Amen.*

Lord, make me an instrument of thy
    peace;
where there is hatred, let me sow love;
where there is injury, pardon;
where there is doubt, faith;
where there is despair, hope;
where there is darkness, light;
and where there is sadness, joy.
O Divine Master,
grant that I may not so much seek
to be consoled as to console;
to be understood as to understand;
to be loved as to love;
for it is in giving that we receive,
it is in pardoning that we are pardoned,
and it is in dying that we are born to
    eternal life.

St. Francis of Assisi

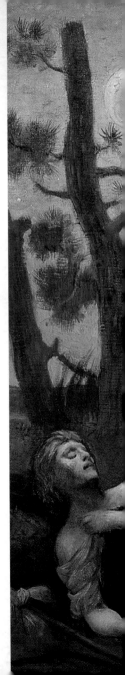

CHAPTER 6

LOVE

✳   ✳   ✳

Neither death, nor life, nor angels, nor rulers, nor things present, nor things to come . . . will be able to separate us from the love of God.

ROMANS 8:38–39

You shall love the Lord your God with all
your heart, and. . . your neighbor as yourself.

Luke 10:27

❋   ❋   ❋

*BECAUSE YOU ARE love, Father, you inspire love in
us all: the love of a friend for a friend, a child for
its parent, the rescued for the rescuer. But even
more than this, Lord, you command us to love our
neighbor as ourselves, and that includes loving our
enemies—an outrageous concept.*

*How can I, a mere human, even fathom a love so
deep that you would sacrifice your only Son for me?
I can't, but I'm still trying, Father. Meanwhile, I
ask you to accept my feeble love in return.*

Love divine, all loves excelling,
joy of heaven, to earth come down,
fix in us thy humble dwelling,
all thy faithful mercies crown.
Jesus, thou art all compassion,
pure, unbounded love thou art;
visit us with thy salvation,
enter every trembling heart.

Breathe, O breathe thy loving Spirit
into every troubled breast;
let us all in thee inherit,
let us find that second rest.
Take away our bent to sinning,
Alpha and Omega be;
end of faith, as its beginning,
set our hearts at liberty.

Finish then thy new creation,
pure and spotless let us be;
let us see thy great salvation,
perfectly restored in thee.
Changed from glory into glory,
till in heaven we take our place,
till we cast our crowns before thee,
lost in wonder, love, and praise!

CHARLES WESLEY, "LOVE DIVINE,
ALL LOVES EXCELLING"

If I have all faith, so as to remove mountains, but do not have love, I am nothing.

1 CORINTHIANS 13:2

❊　　　❊　　　❊

I LOVE MY HUSBAND, Lord. The first time I saw him, I knew he was the one you chose for me. You planted the seed of love within my heart and made it grow and grow and grow. You brought us up together, an unlikely pair, two complete opposites in many ways, and molded us into two halves of the same whole. You made us sweethearts, then best friends, then parents, then grandparents.

We're still easy companions and each other's chief support system—and he still makes me smile. We may not have known what we were doing when we chose each other, but you knew, Lord, and that's what counts.

I believe, God, that you give us faith as a
means of getting in touch with your
love. For once we have that love, we can
pass it on to others.

Love is greater than faith, because the end
is greater than the means. What is the
use of having faith? It is to connect the
soul to God. And what is the object of
connecting man with God? That he
may become like God. But God is
Love. Hence, Faith, the means, is in
order to Love, the end. Love, therefore, obviously is greater than faith. "If
I have all faith, so as to remove mountains, but have not love, I am nothing."

HENRY DRUMMOND
The Greatest Thing in the World

I PRAY FOR ALL the young married people we know. Marriage comes with so many challenges, and they just can't make it work without you, dear God. Keep them focused on you and forgiving of one another. Keep their love strong, and protect them from all evil influences. This is my fervent prayer. Amen.

❈   ❈   ❈

God, the best maker of all marriages,
combine your hearts in one.

WILLIAM SHAKESPEARE

> As a mother comforts her
> child, so I will comfort you.
>
> Isaiah 66:13

❊   ❊   ❊

You changed my world, Father, when you made me a mother. You pulled me and stretched me and taught me servant love. In teaching me how to love my children, you helped me understand the depth of your love for me.

Even though my children are grown, I still experience their pleasures and their pain, and I desire to serve and comfort them. My everlasting gratitude to you, God of love. You have made my life complete.

❊   ❊   ❊

It is no drudgery to serve and comfort those we love.

A friend loves at all times.

PROVERBS 17:17

❋   ❋   ❋

LORD, YOU PAIRED US *up in grade school, my friend and I, though we had little in common. Except for you, we never would have found each other. How did you know that we would pull the best from one another? How could you foresee the adventures we would have?*

When we get together after long absences, the years melt away, and we are kids again. Thank you, Lord, for my wonderful friend. Thank you for the love and laughter and good memories.

❋   ❋   ❋

Friends bring out the best in each other.

Remove the sandals from your feet,
for the place where you stand is holy.

Joseph 5:15

❖   ❖   ❖

In times of struggle, Father, you teach another kind of love: patriotism—love for our country. To each of us, our land is holy ground.

Citizens rally behind their nation whenever trouble bursts in the door. I'm thankful that you have given me a country I can love and serve and be proud of. Continue to bless our citizens and our homeland, Lord. Keep us strong, keep us righteous, keep us close to you.

❖   ❖   ❖

We love our country just because it is our own.

Keep yourselves in the love of God;
look forward to the mercy of our Lord
Jesus Christ that leads to eternal life.

JUDE 21

❋ ❋ ❋

LORD GOD, I OPEN my life to your love.

Help me find you at the depths and heights of my existence.

Shine your light into my dark valleys,

And celebrate with me on the peaks.

Spread your mercy and loving-kindness over me,

So I can walk forever in your paths.

And let the warmth of your eternal love

Cling to me, and radiate to others.

❋ ❋ ❋

Just as our bodies absorb the
warmth of the sun, our souls
absorb the warmth of God's love.

All shall give as they are able, according to the blessing of the Lord your
God that he has given you.

DEUTERONOMY 16:17

❋ ❋ ❋

*YOU HAVE GIVEN me so much, Lord, and I
gladly share my blessings with the poor and
needy. Guide my heart and hands so that
my charity and best intentions reach those
who are truly in need. Make my donations
and gifts of love count, O Lord. Help them
reach their intended destination. Amen.*

❋ ❋ ❋

The best gift is the gift of yourself in the service of another.

By love serve one another.
GALATIANS 5:13 KJV

❊ ❊ ❊

*L*ORD, *I NEVER FULLY* understood your command
to love our neighbors as ourselves and to become
slaves of each other until you gave me a family.
Before that, "self" was always in the way. But
through the years, as you taught me to care for,
comfort, and feed my family, the call to serve
became deeply rooted in my heart. I am happiest
when I serve others, because when I do so I am
serving you, Lord. Thank you for showing me the
joy and beauty in a life of loving service. Amen.

❊ ❊ ❊

To serve others is to serve God.

I reprove and discipline those whom I love.

REVELATIONS 3:19

*L*OVE AND DISCIPLINE *are intertwined in your eyes, Father, but try to convince a child of that. I ask your help as I make and enforce the rules in our home. Help me to be loving and fair as I mete out punishments or consequences. Be my model and my guide, O Lord, as I help my children become the best they can be.*

But I have called you friends, because
I have made known to you everything
that I have heard from my Father.

JOHN 15:15

❊   ❊   ❊

HOW DO I MEASURE the worth of my friends, Father?
As I journey over life's bumps, confronting sorrow and
illness, you provide friends to travel the road with me. As
we eat together, play together, laugh together, you bring
healing of body and mind. Troubles are momentarily
forgotten. You have provided these good friends to share
pleasures and complaints, to give support, comfort,
relaxation, and refreshment. Through this gift of friend-
ship, you help restore my sense of balance and remind
me that you have not abandoned me.

❊   ❊   ❊

Friends double your pleasures
and cut your sorrows in half.

Children are a blessing and a gift from the Lord.

PSALM 127:3 CEV

❊ ❊ ❊

PRAISE TO YOU, O Lord, for the pleasures of grandparenting. I give a little love and get twice as much back. I take my grand-children to the park, the museum, the zoo, and can see life through young eyes again. I can praise their good points, and I don't have to yell at them when they do something dumb. I get to feed them all their favorite foods and leave it up to their parents to feed them the healthy stuff. I can play ball and have fun with them, and never have to force them to do their homework.

I love being a grandmother. It's parenthood without the pain. Motherhood without the muss, fuss, and bother. It's your greatest invention, Lord.

❊ ❊ ❊

Grandchildren make it worth your
while to stick around a few extra years.

And who is my neighbor? . . . The
one who showed . . . mercy.

LUKE 10:29,36

*My NEIGHBOR IS THE FACE of mercy in my life, Lord. She places
the newspaper up on the doorstep where I can reach it. She picks
up my garbage cans when they're rolling in the street. She shovels
my walk on a snowy day. She brings vegetable soup when I don't
feel well enough to cook. These are all tangible reminders of your
love, O Lord. Your face and hands at my door.*

No one has greater love than this, to
lay down one's life for one's friends.

JOHN 15:13

❋   ❋   ❋

*HEADLINES CRY OUT in times of war, Father, of the
sacrifices made by members of our armed forces. These
men and women routinely lay down their lives for the
rest of us. How do we show our thanks? Ceremonies
and words of praise seem so woefully inadequate.*

*Could we, instead, pass on the gift of love and sacrifice
by making small sacrifices of our own on a daily basis?
Could we give our time, our goods, our talents—our
very selves—in the service of others?*

*"Thy will be done," Heavenly Father. Or rather,
"Thy love be done!" Amen.*

And the Lord God planted a garden
in Eden, in the east, and there he put
the man whom he had formed.

GENESIS 2:8

❋　　　❋　　　❋

My GARDEN IS A PLACE of love, dear Father, where my spouse digs and plants and waters, and then awaits your spectacle of beauty that will bring us delight.

You created the first garden, where life began and beauty and love abounded. You are creating still—in our backyards, in parks and fields and forests, and even between the cracks in sidewalks.

How can I possibly deserve such beauty? The answer is, I can't, but I accept your love gift, Lord, in wonder and in joy. Bless my little garden, my little piece of Eden.

❋　　　❋　　　❋

A garden is our closest link to paradise.

How great is the love the Father
has lavished on us, that we should
be called children of God!
1 John 3:1 NIV

❈   ❈   ❈

*Father God, I love how you created earthly relation-
ships to give us a glimpse of our relationship with you.
The love of a parent for a child is the closest we come on
earth to reflecting your unconditional love for us. Most
parents would do anything to keep their children from
harm and raise them in the way they should go—even
when it means disciplining them at times. So it is with all
of us who are your sons and daughters, Lord. As we
experience earthly relationships, we understand more of
how you care for us. Thank you for loving us so much
that you call us your children, and forgive us for those
times we disappoint you. Amen.*

Whoever welcomes one such
child in my name welcomes me.

Matthew 18:5

❋   ❋   ❋

*WHEN I LOOK into the happy eyes of the
children in my life, Lord, my heart aches
for all the impoverished children of the
world for whom life itself is a challenge.
If it is your will, Lord, fill their waiting
hearts with knowledge of you and your
love for them. Please give them shelter,
nourishment, and loving care. Meet their
earthly needs, Lord, that through these
most basic gifts they will know they are
loved. Please reveal to them how precious
they are in your eyes. Amen.*

BLESS THE CHILDREN, *God. Keep them growing in mind and body. Keep them ever moving and reaching out toward the objects of their curiosity. And may they find, in all their explorations, the one thing that holds it all together: your love.*

✻   ✻   ✻

Jesus loves the little children
All the children of the world.
Red and yellow, black and white
They are precious in His sight
Jesus loves the little children of the world.

REV. C. H. WOOLSTON

You shall love the Lord your God
with all your heart, and with all your
soul, and with all your mind. This is
the greatest and first commandment.

MATTHEW 22:37–38

❋   ❋   ❋

*L*ORD, *I* WANT *to love you with all my heart,
soul, and mind as you commanded, but there
are times when, although my heart feels full of
love for you, my mind goes wandering down
another path. My very soul feels heavy and
weary some days, not as light as it should be
if it's only carrying love instead of the world's
burdens. Unite my heart, soul, and mind,
Lord. As they were one at my birth, may they
again be wholly focused on loving you. Amen.*

God is love, and those who abide in love
abide in God, and God abides in them.

1 JOHN 4:16

*M*AY I ENJOY ALL *the streams of love that flow into my life:*

The love from you, God;

The love from family and friends;

The love from parents and children;

The love from pets.

May I celebrate love all day long. For it is the breath of my

existence, and the best of all reasons for living.

I'VE JUST SPENT an afternoon working at home with my cat curled up on my lap, Lord. Typing over her may not be too convenient, but her warm companionship is more than welcome. Thank you for the joy we get from our pets, Lord. Whether fluffy cats, faithful dogs, or curious gerbils, they all bring a measure of love into our lives. We know you created them all, and I just want to say thank you.

All things bright and beautiful,
All creatures great and small,
All things wise and wonderful,
The Lord God made them all.

CECIL FRANCES ALEXANDER

*L*ORD, *I LOVE MY children. They are such a precious gift from you, but mine to hold and shape for only one precious moment in time. Help me remember this during the ordinary rhythm of our days. Keep me mindful in good times and in bad, in joy and in sadness, that it is a sacred trust to be a parent. Thank you for granting me such a gift. Amen.*

❋　　　❋　　　❋

God will redeem in eternity any
time we spend loving a child.

So we have known and believe
the love that God has for us.

1 JOHN 4:16

❋   ❋   ❋

SOME SAY THAT occasionally it's important to stop and take inventory of all that we have. Yet this seems fruitless to me, God, for a couple of reasons. First, I know that all I have is really yours anyway. You gave it to me, and you can take it back anytime you choose. Second, I don't need to take an inventory to know that the most important thing I possess is your love. That's not just something else I need to make my life complete. It's all I need. Thank you for the amazing gift of your love in my life. Amen.

LORD, I AM DRAWN TO the Bible stories of your healing the sick, speaking to the multitudes, and then feeding them with a meager offering of fish and bread. So much of your teaching was in the form of stories, too, Lord, and that's part of why they are so memorable.

I need to remember that you are writing another story through me. It's the story of the life I have as a redeemed person with a living Lord, and because I am saved by your love, the story of my life is a love story. Let me never be ashamed to tell others where I've been and proclaim you as my rescuer. This is my story, my love story, and it is always, only, dedicated to you. Thank you for being the author of my story.

✽   ✽   ✽

What can I give Him, poor as I am?
If I were a shepherd, I would give Him a lamb,
If I were a Wise Man, I would do my part;
Yet what I can give Him: give my heart.
CHRISTINA ROSSETTI, "WHAT CAN I GIVE HIM?"

He will take great delight in you, he
will quiet you with his love, he will
rejoice over you with singing.

ZEPHANIAH 3:17 NIV

❊   ❊   ❊

I DON'T KNOW HOW *I ever get myself into such a dither,
Lord, but there are days when I feel like I just want to scream.
That's when I have to stop, find a quiet place to be alone
with you, and just focus on how much you love me. Knowing that you love me is amazingly comforting. Soon I am
feeling calmed and restored again by your love. Thank you.*

❊   ❊   ❊

Love comforteth like sunshine after rain.

WILLIAM SHAKESPEARE

The Lord watches over all who love him.
PSALM 145:20

❊   ❊   ❊

LORD, THANK YOU so much for the love we get from our families. Even when everyone else abandons us, you made sure we would have someone to love us regardless! Because we have families, we are never truly alone. I praise you for my family and their love for me. Amen.

❊   ❊   ❊

The ones you've given us to love
Are always on our heart.
We pray you'll keep them in your care
Whether near or far apart.

I have loved you with an everlasting love.

JEREMIAH 31:3

❄   ❄   ❄

LORD, I AM GRATEFUL to know there is plenty of love in the world for everyone, every day, because you put it here, and your supply is endless. Thank you for making sure that there will never be a shortage of your love. Amen.

❄   ❄   ❄

To embrace the gifts each day brings is to acknowledge that the Creator never walks away from his creation. Rather, his hand is always at work making us better than we know we can be.

Dear friends, let us practice loving each other, for love comes from God and those who are loving and kind show that they are the children of God, and that they are getting to know him better. But if a person isn't loving and kind, it shows that he doesn't know God—for God is love. God showed how much he loved us by sending His only Son into this wicked world to bring to us eternal life through his death. . . . Dear friends, since God loved us as much as that, we surely ought to love each other too. For though we have never yet seen God, when we love each other God lives in us and his love within us grows ever stronger.

1 John 4:7–10,12 TLB

❊   ❊   ❊

YOU HAVE TOUCHED ME with your love, God. The result is love flowing through me to others. From realizing the depth of your love, my heart longs to show that kind of love to those around me.

For I am convinced that nothing can ever separate us from his love. Death can't, and life can't. The angels won't, and all the powers of hell itself cannot keep God's love away. Our fears for today, our worries about tomorrow, or where we are—high above the sky, or in the deepest ocean— nothing will ever be able to separate us from the love of God demonstrated by our Lord Jesus Christ when he died for us.

Romans 8:38–39 TLB

❄   ❄   ❄

Your love, God, is always reaching out to us, which is cause for celebration. We rejoice in your love every day.

I KNOW THAT YOUR desire for love from us, God, is not primarily for your benefit but for ours. You have taught us that one of your deepest desires is that we know your love, and somehow, when we take action to love you, it is then we discover just how much you love us.

❄   ❄   ❄

God wants us to love him,
not because he is greedy for love,
but because when we are devoted to loving him,
we get in touch with his powerful,
everlasting love for us.
When we do,
we cannot contain it,
and it overflows to others.

For years, God,
I was afraid to approach you—
afraid you'd disapprove of me
or declare me "unacceptable."
When I finally sought you,
I discovered you were tender,
compassionate, loving.

Now, instead of fear,
during my life's purest moments,
I feel secure, embraced,
totally accepted—
and completely loved by you.

❋   ❋   ❋

We sometimes fear drawing close to
God, who is the source of love.
Yet, when we finally choose to draw
near, what a wonderful discovery
we make—we are loved completely.

Love one another, as I have loved you.

John 15:12 KJV

❄   ❄   ❄

I PRAY FOR EVERYONE *to know, God, that you do not love us so that we can hoard your love for ourselves. You desire that we pass it on to others. By spreading the joy of your love, we improve the lives of those around us—and our own lives in the process. Amen.*

❄   ❄   ❄

Real love brings out the best in us. It looks beyond our faults and sees what we can become.

Many waters cannot quench the flame of
love, neither can the floods drown it.

SONG OF SOLOMON 8:7 TLB

❋　　❋　　❋

*L*ORD, WHEN *I am separated from loved*
ones by death, my heart grieves. When I
grieve for these lost ones, I grieve for
myself. Let me celebrate that those who
have gone home to heaven now know
the full essence of your true love. Amen.

❋　　❋　　❋

'Tis better to have loved and lost,
Than never to have loved at all.

ALFRED, LORD TENNYSON, "IN MEMORIAM"

One day I was upon my knees, communing with God upon the subject [of my wife's death], and all at once he seemed to say to me, "You love your wife?" "Yes," I said. "Well, did you love her for her own sake, or yourself? If you loved her for her own sake, why do you sorrow that she is with me? Should not her happiness with me make you rejoice instead of mourn, if you loved her for her own sake? Did you love her," he seemed to say to me, "for my sake? If you loved her for my sake, surely you would not grieve that she is with me. Why do you think of your loss, and lay so much stress upon that instead of thinking of her gain? Can you be sorrowful, when she is so joyful and happy? If you loved her for her own sake, would you not rejoice in her joy, and be happy in her happiness?"

Charles Finney, An Autobiography

It's not hard, Lord, to love those who sparkle—
the diamond people in the world.
The real test of loving is being able to love
those who are like pieces of coal—
those diamonds in the rough who might get us dirty.
But if we love them even so,
with enough positive pressure from love,
one day they'll be diamonds, too!

❋   ❋   ❋

We are naturally drawn to beautiful, kind, loving people. Mature love knows how to love those who seem unlovable, those who seem incapable of giving us anything in return for our love. This kind of love is heaven's love.

Love your enemies! Do good to them!
Lend to them! And don't be concerned
about the fact that they won't repay. Then
your reward from heaven will be very great,
and you will truly be acting as sons of God:
for he is kind to the unthankful and to
those who are very wicked.

LUKE 6:35 TLB

❋   ❋   ❋

*D*EAR *G*OD, *I find that my heart's
capacity is stretched when you tell us to
love our enemies. Yet I know that loving
one's enemies proves that we belong to
you, for you love everyone, no matter
what they have done. I am grateful for
your love, Lord. Amen.*

There is no fear in love. But
perfect love drives out fear.

1 John 4:18

WHEN WE SEE OUR ENEMIES from your perspective, Father, compassion follows, for you have seen the sorrows in their hearts that have caused them to behave in such a manner. I realize you long to reach out to these people and comfort them, and you sometimes use our hands to do it. Help me to understand and to be your hands. Amen.

I love you,
Not only for what you are,
But for what I am
When I am with you.

I love you,
Not only for what
You have made of yourself,
But for what
You are making of me.

I love you because you
Are helping me to make
Of the lumber of my life
Not a tavern
But a temple;
Out of the works
Of my every day
Not a reproach
But a song.

AUTHOR UNKNOWN

I PRAY TO LIVE MY LIFE every day in such a way as to reflect your goodness, God. And I believe I can reflect it most when I love others. It is life's highest and, sometimes, most difficult goal.

❊   ❊   ❊

Friend, you give so much to me:
    a listening ear
    a soothing voice
    a caring heart
    a helping hand
    a healing hug
    a cheering smile.
Thanks for being a loving friend.

*S*OMETIMES LOVE HURTS, *dear Lord, especially when we see loved ones heading for danger. We call to them, "Watch out!" We grab at them and try to bring them back to a safer place. But they don't listen. They break loose, ignoring our warnings. We must stand on safe ground and let them go to learn the hard way.*

Then, if our love is enduring, as yours is, Lord, we stand with open arms to welcome them back when they finally decide: "I am finished with danger—I must go home." And if our love is true, we do not hold to "I told you so" but "I love you—even so."

❊　　❊　　❊

Thinking of our own needs is natural.
Thinking of what others need is supernatural.

LORD, YOU LOVE ME with a faithful love, even when I am unfaithful. May your patience and forgiveness give me confidence and joy, and may I love others as you have loved me. In your holy name, amen.

To be with God, there is no need to be continually in church. We may make [a chapel] of our heart wherein to retire from time to time to converse with him in meekness, humility, and love. There is not in the world a kind of life more sweet and delightful than that of a continual conversation with God.

BROTHER LAWRENCE

O LORD, BE MY HOME. Let me rest in you, live in you, come home to you. I want to abide in your love. Write your commandments on my heart so my greatest desire is to honor you with my life. As I work and play, as I talk and pray, surround all my doings with your energizing presence.

❋   ❋   ❋

Immortal love, forever full,
forever flowing free,
forever shared, forever whole,
a never ebbing sea.

Through him the first fond prayers are said,
our lips of childhood frame;
the last low whispers of our dead
are burdened by his name.

O Lord and master of us all,
whate'er our name or sign,
we own thy sway, we hear thy call
we test our lives by thine.

JOHN GREENLEAF WHITTIER

*D*EAR GOD, HELP *me to love others as you have loved me. Thank you for the privilege of being like your son as I love and serve those around me. Amen.*

❋　　　❋　　　❋

The height to which love exalts is unspeakable. Love unites us to God. Love covers a multitude of sins. Love beareth all things, is long-suffering in all things. There is nothing base, nothing arrogant in love. By love have all the elect of God been made perfect.

CLEMENT OF ROME

Beloved, let us love one another, because love is from God; everyone who loves is born of God and knows God. Whoever does not love does not know God, for God is love.

1 John 4:7–8

❅   ❅   ❅

Lord, let me bask in your awesome love. Let me rest in your presence. I've been away, like the prodigal son, wasting my life in selfish pursuits. But now I'm back, longing to be wrapped in your warm arms. Forgive me, I pray. Welcome me back again. Let me see the dazzling light of your smile as we sit together.

Teach me your wisdom, show me your way, share with me your wants. Remind me again of who I am—and whose I am.

HELP ME LOVE you for yourself, Heavenly Father, and love others as you love me. Change me as you love me, and help me taste the sweetness of your grace. Amen.

❊　　❊　　❊

One there is, above all others,
well deserves the name of Friend;
his is love beyond a brother's,
costly, free, and knows no end;
they who once his kindness prove
find it everlasting love.
Oh, for grace our hearts to soften!
Teach us, Lord, at length to love!
We, alas, forget too often
what a Friend we have above:
but when home our souls are brought
we will love you as we ought.

JOHN NEWTON

Give thanks to the Lord, for he is
good; his love endures forever.

1 CHRONICLES 16:34 NIV

❋   ❋   ❋

*BEFORE I FADE into the welcome arms of sleep, I
want to spend a moment with you, Lord, asking
for your blessing—on my friends and loved ones,
on my church and community, and on myself. You
are a faithful God, strong and true. I am grateful
that you can hear me morning, noon, and night.*

❋   ❋   ❋

Through love to light!
Oh wonderful the way
That leads from darkness
to the perfect day!

RICHARD WATSON GILDER, *After-song*

Holy God, you have shown me light and life.

You are stronger than any natural power.

Accept the words from my heart that
    struggle to reach you.

Accept the silent thoughts and feelings that are
    offered to you.

Clear my mind of the clutter of useless facts.

Bend down to me, and lift me in your arms.

Make me holy as you are holy.

Give me a voice to sing of your love to others.

ANCIENT CHRISTIAN PRAYER, WRITTEN ON PAPYRUS

Love is patient, love is kind. It does not envy, it does not boast, it is not proud.

1 CORINTHIANS 13:4

❄   ❄   ❄

LORD, GO WITH ME today.

Give me your love each step of the way.

Let your presence permeate my work and my play.

Lord, go with me today.

Lord, be with me tomorrow.

Heighten delight and diminish my sorrow.

Where you lead, my dear Lord, I will follow.

Lord, be with me tomorrow.

This is my prayer: that your love
may abound more and more.

PHILIPPIANS 1:9

❊　　❊　　❊

THANK YOU FOR making me in your own image.
See me as you see yourself, Lord, and love me as
you love your own Son. Help me to be more like
you, and guard me as the apple of your eye. Amen.

❊　　❊　　❊

I've found a Friend, O such a Friend!
　He loved me ere I knew him.
He drew me with the cords of love, and
　thus he bound me to him.
And round my heart still closely twine
　those ties which naught can sever,
For I am his and he is mine forever
　and forever.

JAMES G. SMALL

I rely on your constant love; I will be
glad because you will rescue me. I will
sing to you, O Lord, because you
have been good to me.

PSALM 13:6 TEV

❊   ❊   ❊

LORD GOD,

Your love is deeper than the deepest sea.

Your love is higher than the highest star in heaven.

Your grace to me is free—

another unmatchable gift from you to me.

Give me thankfulness for your mercy.

Give me gratitude for your love.

Give me an appreciation of all your gifts—

so freely given to one as undeserving as me.

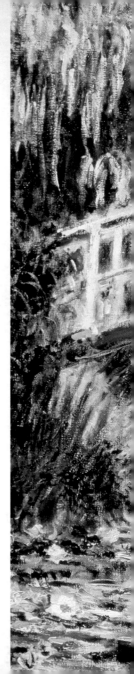

CHAPTER 7

PEACE

The Lord bless you and keep you;
the Lord make his face to shine
upon you . . . and give you peace.

NUMBERS 6:24–26

How very good and pleasant it is
when kindred live together in unity.

PSALM 133:1

❊   ❊   ❊

*LONG AGO I DECIDED, Lord, that I wanted my house
to be a haven of peace for my family. No matter what
happened outside our home, my spouse and children
could find unity and harmony within it.*

*Father, you showed me how to soothe ruffled spirits,
provide an oasis of comfort and solitude, and sow
seeds of pleasure and contentment. Together, we
chased the storms away and created a quiet shelter
where my family could rest and unwind and feel your
love. I thank you, dear Lord, for this gift of peace.*

❊   ❊   ❊

A home should be a fortress
against the storms of the world.

BLESS THIS HOME, LORD. Please fill every heart that lives here with your peace and joy. Make this a home where others enter gladly, feel welcome and loved, and leave refreshed.

Protect this home from disaster and brokenness, Lord, and make it a shelter in the storm for all those who dwell within.

Bless our going out and our coming in from this day forward, and please accept our praise and thanksgiving for this place we are privileged to call home. Amen.

❄   ❄   ❄

This is the true nature of home—it
is the place of Peace; the shelter,
not only from injury, but from all
terror, doubt and division.

JOHN RUSKIN

And let the peace of Christ rule in your hearts . . .

Colossians 3:15

❈ ❈ ❈

Dear God, AT NIGHT as I lie in bed, all the troubles of the day come crowding back into my thoughts unbidden, robbing me of sleep. Up and down the highways of my mind, they travel at a furious pace, colliding and jostling and vying for attention. I call out to you, but no answer comes. Too soon it's dawn, and sleep has still eluded me. Lord of peace, please build for me a quiet chamber in my heart, where I can meet you and find sweet rest.

❈ ❈ ❈

Sleepless nights are
better filled with prayer.

Seek peace and pursue it.
PSALM 34:14

❄   ❄   ❄

Busy, busy, busy. Today's children are so busy, Lord.
They barely have time to breathe. Hurry to catch the
schoolbus . . . hurry to get to classes . . . hurry to get home
and do homework . . . hurry to get to soccer practice or
dance class or music lessons or dental appointments.
The day is gulped down in huge chunks of time, leaving
no room for friends, for relaxation, for dreaming.

Lord, please help us find a less furious pace so our
children can be children once more. Amen.

❄   ❄   ❄

Children are the hands by
which we take hold of heaven.
HENRY WARD BEECHER

PEACE OF MIND, *tranquility—that's what I thought retirement would bring, Lord. But that's a myth. You have shown me that if I choose to feel alive after 55 and continue to serve you, there is action, involvement, commotion, and the occasional emergency. There is fear and anxiety, courage and bravery, grief and sorrow, and there is also joy. A full range of emotions, but no tranquility. Thank you, God.*

Be renewed in the spirit of your minds.

EPHESIANS 4:23

❊   ❊   ❊

LORD, MY LIFE *is a patchwork quilt of bright and dark colors. Each experience and emotion is recorded there. But I long for peaceful spaces in my existence where I can stop to gather up and repair the ragged pieces of my day and stitch them back together. Take me to your place of peace, rest, and renewal, so I may be revived and continue to sew my life's story.*

❊   ❊   ❊

Peace is an island of sweet serenity, where the soul may be refreshed and refueled.

If there is light in the soul, there will be
beauty in the person.

If there is beauty in the person, there will
be harmony in the house.

If there is harmony in the house, there will
be order in the nation.

If there is order in the nation, there will be
peace in the world.

Chinese Proverb

Above all, clothe yourselves with love,
which binds everything together in
perfect harmony. And let the peace
of Christ rule in your hearts.

COLOSSIANS 3:15

❉   ❉   ❉

*F*ATHER, YOU TELL *us that peacemakers are blessed,
but can I be a peacekeeper? Right here in my corner
of the world? As a loving parent, can I keep the
peace among my children, or in my family? Can I
foster harmony among my neighbors? In small
ways? In your name?*

*Show me how, Father. Let your peace rule in my
heart first, then spread out to those I touch.*

❉   ❉   ❉

We can spread the light of peace by lighting
one candle at a time all around the world.

But I say to you, love your enemies and
pray for those who persecute you.

MATTHEW 5:44

❊ ❊ ❊

I CAN LOVE THOSE who love me, Lord—that's the easy part. But
you expect me to reach out further, to those who hate me and
persecute me? You expect me to love my enemies? You promise
great rewards, Father, but I couldn't make peace with thieves or
robbers . . . or terrorists. Could I? But you did. I could only do it
with your help, Lord. Only with your help.

❊ ❊ ❊

Swiftly arose and spread around me the peace and
    knowledge that pass all the argument of the earth,
And I know that the hand of God is the promise
    of my own,
And I know that the spirit of God is the brother
    of my own,
And that all the men ever born are also my brothers,
    and the women my sisters...

WALT WHITMAN

They have treated the wound of my people carelessly,
saying, "Peace, peace," when there is no peace.

JEREMIAH 6:14

❋ ❋ ❋

*Heavenly Father, I often dream of an ideal world, where war
is abolished. But the world is not ideal, and war still exists.*

*You have put peace in my heart, and helped me learn to set aside
anger, but I am only one person. All around me the anger of
others erupts and brushes against me, intruding on my world. I
feel powerless to help. Lord, only you can bring love back to your
world. You alone can accomplish peace. Show me what I can do
to help and let your love shine through.*

❋ ❋ ❋

We look forward to the time when
the power to love will replace the
love of power. Then will our world
know the blessings of peace.

WILLIAM E. GLADSTONE

I CRY OUT TO YOU *for peace in our own country, Father. I see strife everywhere: strife between political parties, between rival companies, between races and religions, and even between schools, neighbors, and family members.*

Lord of life, only you can heal these wounds with your loving touch. Only with your help can our country renew its moral strength. Show me where to begin. Give me cause for hope. Use me, Lord, to spread your gospel of peace.

Hear what God, the Lord, hath spoken:
O my people, faint and few,
Comfortless, afflicted, broken,
Fair abodes I build for you.
Thorns of heart-felt tribulation
Shall no more perplex your ways:
You shall name your walls Salvation,
And your gates shall all be Praise.
There, like streams that feed the garden,
Pleasures without end shall flow;
For the Lord, your faith rewarding,
All his bounty shall bestow;
Still in undisturbed possession
Peace and righteousness shall reign;
Never shall you feel oppression,
Hear the voice of war again.
God shall rise, and, shining o'er you,
Change to day the gloom of night;
He, the Lord, shall be your glory,
God your everlasting light.

WILLIAM COWPER
"THE FUTURE PEACE AND GLORY OF THE CHURCH"

But the wisdom from above is first pure, then peaceable, gentle, willing to yield, full of mercy and good fruits, without a trace of partiality or hypocrisy. And a harvest of righteousness is sown in peace for those who make peace.

JAMES 3:18

❋   ❋   ❋

FATHER GOD, YOU TELL us that to be pure and peaceable is part of being wise. So is gentleness and willingness to yield. These sound like the attributes of a good mediator, Lord. Please give us this kind of wisdom. Bestow on our country's ambassadors those qualities that can reap a harvest of peace. Be with them on their peace missions, Lord, as they attempt to put out the fires of war throughout the world.

❋   ❋   ❋

Five enemies of peace inhabit with us— avarice, ambition, envy, anger, and pride; if these were to be banished, we should infallibly enjoy perpetual peace.

PETRARCH

But when I looked for good, evil came;
and when I waited for light, darkness
came. My inward parts are in turmoil and
are never still; days of affliction come to
meet me. I go about in sunless gloom.

JOB 30:26–28

✳ ✳ ✳

THESE WORDS OF JOB concerning his inner turmoil are like those of my friend, who is besieged with trouble on every side. She tries so hard to handle her problems with integrity and grace, but the troubles just keep multiplying. Her prayers seem to go unanswered. I've tried to be of help. I've tried to ease her pain, but only you can do that, Lord. Please take away her relentless darkness and help her to find the sunlight of your peace again. Amen.

✳ ✳ ✳

The beauty of the dawn follows even the darkest night.

*L*ORD, THANK YOU *for my nurse. He soothes and calms with his words and manner, which is every bit as important as the medicines he dispenses. Please bless my nurse, Lord, and bless all nurses everywhere, who help to bring your peace to frightened patients.*

❈   ❈   ❈

My prayers for you always include an angel
or two, because that's what you are to me.

I will lie down and sleep in peace, for you alone, O Lord, make me dwell in safety.

PSALM 4:8 NIV

❊   ❊   ❊

WHEN I'M SO TIRED that I don't think I can finish one more task, I thank you, God, for drawing the day to an end. I praise you for providing the safe shelter of my home, a warm bath, a cozy bedroom, and a pillow on which to lay my head. Thank you, Lord, for tucking me in surrounded by your love. Amen.

❊   ❊   ❊

Have courage for the great sorrows of life and patience for the small ones; and when you have laboriously accomplished your daily task, go to sleep in peace. God is awake.

VICTOR HUGO

Peace I leave with you; my peace I give to you.

JOHN 14:27

❋   ❋   ❋

GOD, THOSE WHO *say there is no peace in the world haven't been paying attention to all the wonderful things around them. There is peace in the way a cloud drifts effortlessly across a blue sky. There is peace in the sound of a brook trickling over smooth, round rocks in a woodland stream, and in the almost silent sighs of a newborn baby sleeping. Quiet my heart, O Lord, so I may sense and rest in the peacefulness you have placed in the world.*

❋   ❋   ❋

We shall find peace. We shall hear the angels, we shall see the sky sparkling with diamonds.

ANTON CHEKHOV

*Y*OU HAVE GIVEN US *the only hope for eternal peace—the peace that passes all human understanding, Father God. By sending your Son to die on the cross for our sins, you made it possible for all who accept him as Lord and Savior to have the peace that can only come with the assurance of eternal life. In times of trial and heartache, it is to that peace we turn—to that peace we often run. Thank you, God, for finding a way to close the gap between you and us—and for the eternal peace that is ours to claim. Amen.*

In quietness and in trust shall be your strength.

ISAIAH 30:15

❈   ❈   ❈

*L*ORD, WHY IS IT *I so often feel the need to fill the silence with chatter or noise? When I'm with a friend who just needs my presence, not my advice, let me be comfortable with the lulls in our conversation. Let me realize we may both need the opportunity to gather our thoughts. When I'm driving in the car, remind me to use the silence to pray to you. At times when I'm busy at home, stop me from filling the silence with a blaring television or radio.*

I know I shouldn't fear silence, Lord, for it's when my heart is quiet that I can hear you most clearly. Help me learn to rejoice in silence!

Those who live according to the Spirit set their minds on the things of the Spirit. . . . to set the mind on the Spirit is life and peace.

Romans 8:5–6

❄ ❄ ❄

WHAT PEACE WE get from the message of Easter, Father. It is the best proof we have that you keep your promises. Thank you for assuring us that death is not the end, that your Son did indeed go to prepare a place for us more magnificent than anything we can imagine. Let me be like the women at Jesus' empty tomb, eager to run and spread the news! Amen.

❄ ❄ ❄

It isn't necessary to pray in order for God to know what's on our minds—he already knows. We pray so we will know what's on God's mind.

He will feed his flock like a shepherd; he will
gather the lambs in his arms, and carry them in
his bosom, and gently lead the mother sheep.

Isaiah 40:11

❊   ❊   ❊

*Lord, I see lots of people on a frantic search for peace in
their lives. Some think escaping daily demands is the answer.
They believe that by getting as far away from their responsi-
bilities as they can they will find peace. Satisfy the searching
in these people's souls, Lord. Please reveal yourself to them
in a way they can understand so that, after a lifetime of
looking everywhere else, they will see you and know peace.*

❊   ❊   ❊

Never be in a hurry; do everything quietly
and in a calm spirit. Do not lose your
inner peace for anything whatsoever, even
if your whole world seems upset.

St. Francis de Sales

Great peace have those who love your
law; nothing can make them stumble.

PSALM 119:165

❀   ❀   ❀

*HELP ME TO REMEMBER that if I am to feel peaceful then I have
to be full of your peace, O Lord. And I can't be full of your peace
unless I spend time in your presence.*

*Grant that I seek you first when my world seems to be spinning
out of control and feels anything but peaceful. Help me to empty
myself of all the anxieties and worries that rob me of your peace.
Give me a heart to seek you first, Lord, to know your peace, and
to let it radiate from me to all those around me.*

As is so often prayed, make me an instrument of your peace.

❀   ❀   ❀

Where there is peace, God is.

GEORGE HERBERT

Keep on doing the things that you have learned and received and heard and seen in me, and the God of peace will be with you.

PHILIPPIANS 4:9

❋　　❋　　❋

LORD GOD, AS I look back on my life, grant me the peace that comes from knowing I wouldn't change any part of it even if I could. For you have given me the courage to endure every trial and the wisdom to know everything works together for good. True peace comes from leaving it all in your hands, Lord, and so I do.

❋　　❋　　❋

Peace puts forth her olive everywhere.

WILLIAM SHAKESPEARE

The Lord bless you and keep you; the Lord make his face to shine upon you, and be gracious to you; the Lord lift up his countenance upon you, and give you peace.

NUMBERS 6:24–26

❊　　　❊　　　❊

PARENTS HAVE SO many things to worry them and keep them awake at night, Lord. Concerns about coughs and sneezes and falls and scratches often haunt mothers and fathers. Give parents your peace, Lord. Calm their hearts with the message that their children are in your hands, and you will never let them be taken away from you. I ask this in your precious name, amen.

❊　　　❊　　　❊

Bless our little ones today;
Bid your angels close to stay.
Protect them, Lord, as all the while
We see you in each sweet smile.

*F*ATHER, THERE WAS SO much anxiety when we entered a new millennium. Some even said that the world as we knew it was coming to an end. A lot of time has passed since then, and our world is still intact. Help us to remember that you existed long before our world came into being, and you will exist into eternity. Give us your peace throughout time, O God, for you are the rock of ages.

There is a river whose streams
make glad the city of God, the holy
habitation of the Most High.

PSALM 46:4

❊   ❊   ❊

*I WANT PEACE TO BE more than a spiritual goal for me,
Lord, I want it to be a lifestyle. When I awake in the morning and lie down at night, let your peace flow over me.
When everything seems chaotic around me, let me respond
peacefully. I know I can't do that without you, Lord. Please
grant me an abundance of your peace. Amen.*

❊   ❊   ❊

Where the soul is full of peace and joy,
outward surrounding and circumstances
are of comparatively little account.

HANNAH WHITEHALL SMITH

Ere we reach the shining river,
Lay we every burden down;
Grace our spirits will deliver,
And provide a robe and crown.
    Yes, we'll gather at the river,
    The beautiful, the beautiful river—
    Gather with the saints at the river
    That flows by the throne of God.
Soon we'll reach the shining river,
Soon our pilgrimage will cease,
Soon our happy hearts will quiver
With the melody of peace.
    Yes, we'll gather at the river,
    The beautiful, the beautiful river—
    Gather with the saints at the river
    That flows by the throne of God.

ROBERT LOWRY, "BEAUTIFUL RIVER"

So he came and proclaimed peace to you who
were far off and peace to those who were near.

EPHESIANS 2:17

❋   ❋   ❋

*L*ORD, I KNOW THAT *peace of mind is mine for the asking,
but so often I let worry about things that will never even
happen rob me of the peace you intend for me to have.
Teach me to keep those thoughts at bay, Lord. When they
do enter my mind, grant me the wisdom to immediately
replace them with thoughts of your power, your grace, and
your mercy. Remind me of the lilies of the field and the
birds of the air and how you care for them. I know you
came to the world to bring us peace, Lord, and that you left
it for us as a precious gift. Help me claim that gift day after
day, regardless of what my circumstances may be.*

For the kingdom of God is . . . righteousness and peace and joy in the Holy
Spirit. . . . Let us then pursue what makes
for peace and for mutual upbuilding.

Romans 14:17,19

❋   ❋   ❋

*WHERE CAN WE FIND your peace, Lord? Should we go to the
forest and sit on a rock under a big tree? Or would a stroll on a
long, deserted beach reveal it to us? Should we try to legislate,
orchestrate, or negotiate it? We've made it harder than you
meant for it to be, Lord. Please turn us in the direction of your
simple, perfect peace—and the sooner the better.*

❋   ❋   ❋

First keep the peace within yourself, then
you can also bring peace to others.

Thomas à Kempis

GOD, *I* KNOW THAT YOU *want me to know peace in every area of my life—peace in my daily work, peace in my business, peace in my family, peace in my soul. The key to letting peace enter in is to invite you into each of these areas daily. So I extend to you my most sincere prayer invitation to accompany me every day. Amen.*

The name of peace is sweet, and the thing itself is beneficial. . . . Peace is freedom in tranquility.

MARCUS TULLIUS CICERO

Therefore, beloved, while you are waiting for these things, strive to be found by him at peace, without spot or blemish; and regard the patience of our Lord as salvation.

2 Peter 3:14–15

❊ ❊ ❊

I FEEL ANGRY AT so many people, Lord. Often I think my life would be peaceful if only they would just do the right thing. I convince myself they are robbing me of peace, but at this moment I know it's my choice to let go of anger and embrace peace. Staying angry at them for not living up to my expectations doesn't solve any problems; it just creates new ones. Please help me to remember that "anger does not bring about the righteous life that God desires" (James 1:19, NIV), in me or in those I'm staying angry at. Give me strength to release them so I can go back to that serene, tranquil place called "peace."

I . . . beg you to lead a life worthy of the
calling to which you have been called, with
all humility and gentleness, with patience,
bearing with one another in love, making
every effort to maintain the unity of the
Spirit in the bond of peace.

EPHESIANS 4:1–3

❊ ❊ ❊

I BELIEVE WE CAN DECIDE *to be at peace with the state of our
lives, Almighty God. Help us to avoid falling into the rut of
constantly desiring more and better things and positions rather
than being content with what we have. Otherwise, we may never
know your peace. In your name I pray. Amen.*

❊ ❊ ❊

Perhaps we need to rethink our idea of what
"peace" really is. God is always ready to give us
true peace, if we are willing to ask him for it.

Fix your thoughts on what is true and good and right. Think about things that are pure and lovely, and dwell on the fine, good things in others. Think about all you can praise God for and be glad about. Keep putting into practice all you learned from me and saw me doing, and the God of peace will be with you.

PHILIPPIANS 4:8–9 TLB

❈   ❈   ❈

A LOT OF PEOPLE TALK about love and peace, Lord, but it can be difficult to put words into action. We live in a world that celebrates talk. Talk fills the airwaves on the radio and on television. All the talking is well and good, but the true test comes when it's time to take out the trash. Sure, it can feel great to talk about love and peace, but ultimately love is something we do to help accomplish peace. Keep me mindful of not just talking but also doing, dear God. Amen.

❈   ❈   ❈

When we focus on the negative, peace eludes us. But positive thinking leads to peace.

Don't worry about anything; instead, pray about everything; tell God your needs and don't forget to thank him for his answers. If you do this you will experience God's peace, which is far more wonderful than the human mind can understand. His peace will keep your thoughts and your hearts quiet and at rest as you trust in Christ Jesus.

Philippians 4:6–7 TLB

❅   ❅   ❅

In many different relationships, dear God, I have found the elements of what makes me feel at home:

> *in the conversation of close friends,*
> *in the smiles of helpful neighbors,*
> *in the laughter of family celebrations,*
> *and especially in the peace of your presence.*

Wherever you have sprinkled love, joy, peace, patience, kindness, goodness, faithfulness, and gentleness, there I have discovered a place for my soul to rest, a place to call home.

*S*OMETIMES, *FATHER, I need to go outdoors to seek a place where I can find tranquility and peace. In such a delightful place, I listen to the musical sounds of nature and observe the beauty of your creation. I converse with you in prayer and am reassured to know you are still in control. Thank you for soothing me with your strength and your love. Amen.*

But all who humble themselves before
the Lord shall be given every blessing
and shall have wonderful peace.

PSALM 37:11 TLB

❊   ❊   ❊

*PEACE IS ABOUT releasing. It's about opening my hand
and letting go of my plan, my agenda, and my demands
on you, God, on other people, and even on myself.*

*It's about realizing that, in your eyes, every person is as
important as I am. It's remembering I don't know everything, and I don't have solutions to every problem.*

It's about calling on you, Lord, the one who does.

❊   ❊   ❊

The meaning I picked, the one that changed
my life: Overcome fear, behold wonder.

AESCHYLUS

My child, do not let these escape from
your sight: keep sound wisdom and prudence, and they will be life for your soul
and adornment for your neck. . . . If you
sit down, you will not be afraid; when you
lie down, your sleep will be sweet.

PROVERBS 3:21–22,24

❈ ❈ ❈

I TOSS AND TURN, *God of nighttime peace, making lists of
"must do" and "should have done . . . or not" and wind up
feeling unequal to the tasks and sleep-deprived to boot.
Bless me with deep sleep and dreams that reveal me as you
see me: beloved, worthy, capable.*

*At dawn, help me see possibilities on my lists. Each time I
yawn today, Lord—for it was a short night—I'll breathe in
your restorative presence and exhale worries. Tonight I'll
sleep like the sheep of your pasture, for I lie down and rise
up in your care—restored, renewed, and rested. Amen.*

Live in harmony with one another; do not be haughty, but associate with the lowly; do not claim to be wiser than you are. Do not repay anyone evil for evil, but take thought for what is noble in the sight of all. If it is possible, so far as it depends on you, live peaceably with all.

ROMANS 12:16–18

❊   ❊   ❊

Bless me with the kind heart of a peacemaker and a builder's sturdy hand, Lord, for these are mean-spirited, litigious times when we tear down with words and weapons first and ask questions later. Help me take every opportunity to compliment, praise, and applaud as I rebuild peace.

❊   ❊   ❊

Heaven is not reached at a single bound;
But we build the ladder by which we rise
From the lowly earth to the vaulted skies,
And we mount to its summit round by round.

JOSIAH GILBERT HOLLAND

FATHER, I CELEBRATE the gift of contentment, knowing there is no guarantee it will last. But for now, it's great to rest—just to rest—in this wonderful calm. Thank you, Lord.

❊   ❊   ❊

Peace and rest at length have come
All the day's long toil is past,
And each heart is whispering, "Home,
Home at last."

THOMAS HOOD

HEAVENLY FATHER, I know we all make plans for our lives and have an agenda we want to hold on to. Yet if we let go of this agenda and let you be in charge, the result will bring us peace. Help me learn how to let go so I may bask in your peace. Amen.

❄   ❄   ❄

Like a river glorious is God's perfect peace,
Over all victorious in its bright increase;
Perfect, yet it floweth fuller every day,
Perfect, yet it groweth deeper all the way.
Ev'ry joy or trial falleth from above,
Traced upon our dial by the sun of love;
We may trust him fuller all for us to do—
They who trust him wholly find him wholly true.
Stayed upon Jehovah, hearts are fully blest—
Finding, as he promised, perfect peace and rest.

FRANCES RIDLEY HAVERGAL
"LIKE A RIVER GLORIOUS"

Whatever house you enter, first say,
"Peace to this house!" And if anyone
is there who shares in peace, your
peace will rest on that person.

LUKE 10:5–6

❋   ❋   ❋

LET YOUR PEACE rest upon our home, dear God.

Help us to love one another as you have loved us.

We fail to reach out the way you have gathered us in.

We forget how to give when only taking fills our minds.

And, most of all, we need your presence to know we are more

than just parents and children.

We are always your beloved sons and daughters.

Let your peace rest upon our home, dear God.

❋   ❋   ❋

He is happiest, be he king or peasant,
who finds peace in his home.

JOHANN WOLFGANG VON GOETHE

Those of steadfast mind you keep in peace—in peace because they trust in you. Trust in the Lord forever, for in the Lord God you have an everlasting rock.

ISAIAH 26:3–4

❅   ❅   ❅

YOU HAVE PROMISED, dear God, that you will keep me in perfect peace when I fix my thoughts on you. I know from experience that this principle of peace holds true as I face all kinds of challenges.

When David kept his focus on how great you are, Goliath fell. Likewise, when I remain calm, placing my trust in you, my biggest problems are cut down to size. Thank you for the many times and ways in which you have helped me continue to learn this life lesson. Increase my peace, I pray, Lord, as I trust you. Amen.

All this is from God, who reconciled us
to himself through Christ, and has given
us the ministry of reconciliation.

2 Corinthians 5:18

❄   ❄   ❄

CONTENTION AND friction in family relationships leave me feeling uneasy, Lord. I long for reconciliation and peace, but I don't know how to make it happen. Help me to do my part in this matter, whether it means speaking the truth in love to someone, letting go of something, seeking or offering forgiveness, praying, or quietly setting an example. Show me how to walk in your way of peace, God, and let that peace permeate each relationship in my life.

❄   ❄   ❄

Be known to us in breaking bread,
But do not then depart;
Saviour, abide with us, and spread
Thy table in our heart.

James Montgomery, "The Family Table"

I will heal my people and will
let them enjoy abundant peace.

JEREMIAH 33:6

✳   ✳   ✳

*G*OD OF PEACE, WHAT *are we to do with our anger? In the wake
of trouble, it fills us to overflowing. Sometimes our anger is the
only prayer we can bring you. We are relieved and grateful to know
that you are sturdy enough to bear all we feel and say. Where do we
go from here? Is there life after fury? What will we be without
our anger when it's all that has fueled us? When we are still, we
hear your answer: "Emptied." But then we would be nothing.*

*Remind us that, in your redeeming hands, Father, "nothing" can
become of great use, as a gourd hollowed out becomes a cup or a
bowl only when emptied. When the time comes for us to empty
ourselves of this abundance of anger, make us into something
useful. In your name I pray. Amen.*

For wisdom will come into your heart, and
knowledge will be pleasant to your soul;
prudence will watch over you; and understanding will guard you.

PROVERBS 2:10–11

※　　　※　　　※

*B*LESSINGS UPON US.

The blessing of perfect acceptance in the face of daunting
circumstances.

The blessing of contentment and peace while the winds blow and
the waves rise higher and higher.

The blessing of discernment:

to recognize when to wait, and to understand when to move.

※　　　※　　　※

You have made us for yourself and our
hearts are restless until they rest in you.

ST. AUGUSTINE OF HIPPO
Confessions of St. Augustine

He made the storm be still, and the waves of the sea were hushed. Then they were glad because they had quiet, and he brought them to their desired haven. Let them thank the Lord for his steadfast love, for his wonderful works to humankind.

Psalm 107:29–31

❄   ❄   ❄

THE UNKNOWN FRIGHTENS me sometimes, God, and right now my life is so uncertain. How can I know what to do when I don't know what will happen next? How do I know what you intend by this?

I know this is one of those faith–stretching experiences, but I don't feel up to the challenge right now. Please bring your calm to my anxious thoughts; bring your peace to the turmoil in my emotions. You are far bigger than any challenge I will ever face in life. Let this reality be a starting point for my growing trust in your goodness.

❄   ❄   ❄

A crust eaten in peace is better than a banquet partaken in anxiety.

Aesop

Let me hear what God the Lord will speak,
for he will speak peace to his people, to his
faithful, to those who turn to him in their
hearts. . . . Steadfast love and faithfulness
will meet; righteousness and peace will kiss
each other. . . . Righteousness will go before
him, and will make a path for his steps.

Psalm 85:8,10,13

❊   ❊   ❊

O LORD, HEAR my prayer.

Remind me that you are always with me.

Fill me with your peace,

grant me your mercy,

and lead me in your ways.

In your name I pray, amen.

❊   ❊   ❊

Peace can . . . be reached through concentration
upon that which is dearest to the heart.

Patanjali

The greatest burden that we have to carry in life is self. The most difficult thing we have to manage is self. . . . In laying off your burdens therefore, the first one you must get rid of is yourself. You must hand yourself and all your inward experiences, your temptations, your temperament, your . . . feelings all over into the care and keeping of our God. And leave them there. He made you, He understands you, He knows how to manage you, and you must trust Him to do it.

HANNAH WHITEHALL SMITH
The Christian's Secret to a Happy Life

I PRAISE YOU FOR THE blue sky, the comforting breeze, and the rustle of leaves, O Lord. Nature is so remarkable. When you created the earth, you thought of every detail. Every color is so perfect, each sound so peaceful. The lapping water of the shoreline lulls me to sleep, the gorgeous sunrise wakes me in the morning, and the beauty of all that surrounds me gives me peace during the day. Thank you for your artistry. I enjoy it so very much. Amen.

*   *   *

Peace is always beautiful.

WALT WHITMAN

The effect of righteousness will be
peace, and the result of righteousness,
quietness and trust forever.

ISAIAH 32:17

❋　　　❋　　　❋

*FATHER IN HEAVEN, thank you for teaching me to be content;
it certainly saves a lot of time that might otherwise be spent
complaining. The inner peace I have is one of the many gifts
from you. And the moral strength that you instilled in me
has carried me through many otherwise destructive times.
You are indeed a God of practicality and love.*

❋　　　❋　　　❋

He who does not attempt to make peace
when small discords arise is like the
bee's hive which leaks drops of honey.
Soon, the whole hive collapses.

SIDDHA NAGARJUNA

My soul, there is a country
Afar beyond the stars,
Where stands a winged sentry
All skillful in the wars;
There, above noise and danger
Sweet Peace sits, crown'd with smiles,
And One born in a manger
Commands the beauteous files.
He is thy gracious Friend
And (O my soul awake!)
Did in pure love descend,
To die here for thy sake.
If thou canst get but thither,
There grows the flow'r of Peace,
The Rose that cannot wither,
Thy fortress, and thy ease.
Leave then thy foolish ranges,
For none can thee secure,
But One who never changes,
Thy God, thy life, thy cure.

HENRY VAUGHAN, "PEACE"

ACKNOWLEDGMENTS

✻ ✻ ✻

PICTURE CREDITS

❊   ❊   ❊